LIVING
YOUNGER

DISCOVER THE SECRETS TO ENJOYING A YOUNG BODY,
SPIRIT, AND MIND AT ANY AGE

LIVING YOUNGER

DISCOVER THE SECRETS TO ENJOYING A YOUNG BODY, SPIRIT, AND MIND AT ANY AGE

ANGELA MYERS

TABLE OF CONTENTS

INTRODUCTION

*"Nobody grows old by living a number of years.
We grow old by deserting our ideals."*
–Samuel Ullman

Aging is inevitable, but growing "old" is a choice. Aging happens to us every day and has happened to us from the moment we entered the world. Our early years were spent yearning for our next birthday, yearning to be old enough and big enough for new privileges, and dreaming about "growing up". For many people, this enthusiasm for getting older fades and becomes replaced with a fear or a dread of aging.

Have you noticed a decline in your physique, ease of movement, energy levels, or zest for life over the past few years? Have you begun to dread aging? Are you ready to create a future that you look forward to? Would you like to create an amazing aging experience? Then this book is for you!

You will learn that your age is not related to a number, rather, age is something you experience. Embracing the perspective of age as an experience opens up an empowering realm of possibility, where you can CHOOSE your experience! After reading this book, you will feel renewed enthusiasm for the years to come! You will feel empowered to create an aging process you feel good about, as you become aware that **many aspects of the aging process are within your control**! You will learn of some changes you can make in your daily routine that will allow you to live with vitality for decades to come. I want to gift you with the confidence that you can take actions today to stay young tomorrow.

I bring a unique perspective to this topic as a life coach who also is a leader in the fitness industry. I have studied a broad range of being human. I studied human behavior and psychology, as I started my career with a degree in Social Work. Then I studied the human body as I became a personal trainer when I was in my late 20's. I opened a personal training facility, and over the next decade I observed and trained hundreds of people while I continued to learn from the world's best teachers in the fields of nutrition, metabolism, fitness, and the movement of human body (kinesiology). I observed the way our emotions and thoughts effect our behavior choices, which then effects the condition of our bodies. I then expanded my studies to become a life coach so that I could help people experience even deeper levels of well-being as we could now integrate emotional and spiritual health. I respect the intimate connection between the mind, body, and spirit.

My concept of being an older adult was completely reshaped the first time I participated in a Master's Track and Field National Championships event. When I arrived at the competition, my mind was blown by what I saw before me. There were men and women competing in all the track and field events, starting at age 35 up to ages 70, 80, 90, even 100 years old! Athletes were warming up all around the stadium, and the event on the track when I arrived was women's hurdles, age group 70-75. I was astonished to see these older women leaping over hurdles at full speed! As amazed as I was to see older athletes competing at this level, I was equally amazed to see how young they looked! For example, when they would call Men's 100m onto the track and announce, "Age group 60-65", the men that stepped out looked like they were in their early 50's or even younger! As I sat beside my friend, watching the events of that first day, she pointed out one of her teammates across the field who sprinted up to the high jump bar and cleared it effortlessly. She was a lean athletic woman with a light-colored ponytail. Watching her move from across the track, I assumed she was in her late 30's. When I met her in person, I learned she was in her early 60's! Since then, I have witnessed athletes as old as 103 setting world records! I have seen hundreds of men and women in their 70's, 80's, and 90's maintaining focused workout regimens and competing at high levels. What had these athletes discovered that allowed them to enjoy such a high quality of life, and seemingly reverse aging by 1-2 decades?

I've engaged with this question over the past ten years, and while closely observing and studying all aspects of the human experience I've discovered that there are many factors of aging within our control! In observing the hundreds of individuals I trained in my studio and in Masters sports, I saw confirmation in case after case that one's age number did not correspond to the level of youth in one's body!

The purpose of this book is to empower you to create an amazing aging experience! I will teach you the secrets of youth and how to apply them so that you will not "grow old" if you don't want to! I will equip you with information, tools, and resources that will enable you to create a compelling future. You will learn how to make the small habits, actions, and lifestyle changes that will allow you to enjoy life feeling a decade younger than your chronological age!

This book is designed to serve as a guide, to lead you to concepts and to help you do your own research. I will skim the surface of many aspects of vitality and give you resources for further investigation, as there are already many good books, articles, and research studies that will delve deeper into these concepts.

If you are in your 30's or 40's, you can use this knowledge preventatively, so that you do not experience aging at the rate of the majority of the population. If you are in your 50-70's, you will be able to use these concepts to reverse your body age. Many older clients that I coached received compliments from their friends and family about how they were looking younger, as changes were happening in all cells of their body that affected their skin, posture, energy levels, muscle tone, and libido. Included in this book are inspirational examples of people who did not start their journey until their 60's and 70's.

Within this book, you will find that I address you as a whole Human Being. Many books segment various components of being a human, writing only about nutrition, or solely about exercise and workouts, or maybe a book with a focus on spirituality. In this book, I put all aspects together so that you have a holistic perspective on how to be a younger human! We are so beautifully and intricately designed, that it would be a disservice not to integrate all aspects.

Life is best measured by the *quality* of your years, not the *quantity*. A youthful heart, a youthful soul, and a youthful body—these all need to be united to experience life to the fullest! As Abraham Lincoln said, "In the end, it is not the years in your life that count. It's the life in your years."

So with love and all my positive intentions for a rich life ahead, I give you the secrets to living younger!

CHAPTER 1:
THE POWER OF THE MIND

"Whether you think you can or you think you can't, you're right."
–Henry Ford

A youthful body age starts with the belief that you can have one! What expectations have you set for yourself if you project yourself forward 20 years? Take a few minutes to become aware of how you imagine yourself to be; it is hidden in your unconscious beliefs and will show itself! Close your eyes, and picture yourself in 20 years. In your projection, what does your body look like? How are you moving? What activities are you doing? Ultimately, whatever hidden "expectations" you have about what you will be like is **what will manifest and become your reality**. The mind is very powerful and uses our projections and expectations like a GPS. If your projection shows you as an 80-year-old with stooped posture, bony and frail, sitting in an EZ chair watching TV, then that is programmed to be your destiny!

But what if you changed that projected expectation? What if you saw yourself in your 80's, wearing a bathing suit while enjoying a sunrise walk on an exotic beach?

Living Proactively vs. Reactively

Challenging your expectations may create some inner tension initially, as it is often our first response to resist the confrontation of our deeply held beliefs. Often we are not even aware of these beliefs as they are hidden in the subconscious part of our minds. Our minds have built solid reasons for why we can or cannot do certain things, or why it might be ridiculous to expect ourselves to be skipping around on a beach when we're 80. When we challenge a limiting belief, we open ourselves up to replace it with a new, empowering belief.

You have the opportunity to take control of your mindset, to proactively program your own "destiny GPS". This means switching from a **Reactive** mindset to a **Proactive** mindset. The reality is that if YOU do not proactively choose your thoughts and expectations about your aging process, you will ride on the GPS autopilot that your culture has set for you. These expectations are programmed in your subconscious mind. If left unexposed or unchallenged, you will embody the mindsets and lifestyles of those closest to you, the media you are influenced by, and the cultural norms around you. Exposing (becoming aware of) your expectations of being an older adult is what empowers you to CHOOSE your aging process rather than accept the one you've been conditioned to expect.

Living reactively means living in victim mode, where you feel "Life happens to me". Living proactively means living in empowered mode, where you understand "Life happens BY me".

When you live in reactive mode, your life is a series of reactions to events and circumstances that you feel powerless to control. Your area of personal focus tends to be on things you can't control, such as the stock market, your boss, your kids, your spouse, other people's opinions, world events, and politics, to name a few. Because there is so much focus on what you CANNOT control, there is little energy left to be given to what you CAN control.

> *"The moment you take responsibility for everything in your life is the moment you can change anything in your life"*
> –Hal Elrod

When you live in proactive mode, you shift your focus and personal energy to things YOU can control. These are things like your mindset, your feelings, your health, your nutrition, your performance at work, your parenting skills, your decisions, your investment in your spouse. You take responsibility for yourself instead of blaming other people or circumstances for the state of your well-being or the quality of your life. You make decisions and take actions on what you need and want, and because you are now being proactive, your life takes the direction YOU want it to go.

I challenge you to take a proactive approach to your aging experience! While there are some factors regarding aging that you cannot control, there are far more factors that you can control! Accepting this truth—that you are not a victim to the way you age (a reactor), but rather **you are RESPONSIBLE for the way that you age**—is the most empowering concept in this book.

Let's think about the Proactive vs. Reactive mindset concept through the lens of a lifestyle disease. Heart Disease, a lifestyle disease, is the leading cause of death in the United States. If you were living with a Reactive mindset, you would cruise through 4-5 decades perhaps too busy to work out regularly, keeping a stressful job to make sure the family has what they need, giving some thought to your diet, but many times just grabbing food on the road between obligations or skipping meals. One day, you experience a minor heart attack, and you feel victimized. You are shocked and angry that this would happen to you, and you spend the next several weeks, months, and years reacting to this setback (time off work, perhaps heart surgery, taking medications, modifying the activities you are able to enjoy).

With a Pro-active mindset, you take control of your lifestyle *before* tragedy strikes. You set your focus on the areas you can control and give them your best energy. This requires making hard choices, but you make them because you know what you want and need. Proactive mode is setting the alarm earlier to exercise or meditate every day, packing and planning nutrient filled foods for your meals every day, sacrificing junk activities for higher living activities, and saying "no" to requests (even if they are good and noble requests) that may drain your energy or take time away from the activities that bring life to you. Living in this way, you would experience high levels of wellness and energy, and eliminate many risk factors that have been proven to cause heart attacks. Proactive living is about focusing on what you CAN control (your diet, your lifestyle, your thoughts, your stress levels, your sleep) and letting go of what you CANNOT control (genetics).

There is an element of living proactively that may feel selfish to people who are givers, or who are others-conscious. I am a giver, and I always will be a giver. I was raised to think that putting myself first was selfish and even sinful! In my community, others came first. To be the last, to be the one to sacrifice, was not only good, it was Godly! While this is a beautiful concept, this belief fails to create healthy givers who sacrifice with freedom rather than obligation and guilt. I am learning to focus on being full of energy and life first, and then to give from that abundance! If you are at your best, if you are healthy and happy and full of energy, ONLY THEN can you give sustainably and in amazing ways to your loved ones and community. Reacting to everyone else's needs as a first priority will work for a few decades but eventually you will be physically, emotionally, and spiritually unable to give as much as you want.

> *"Don't ask what the world needs. Ask what makes you come alive, and go do it! Because what the world needs is people who have come alive."*
> –Howard Thurman

If you resist prioritizing your needs (ex: sleep, exercise, meditation, healthy nutrition, a life-giving hobby) and instead hold other people's needs and goals higher, you will age rapidly. I invite you to renew your focus on restoring your body, mind, and soul! I have seen so many generous, caring, beautiful people put their self-care last in the interest of living out the needs and expectations of others. They end up in my office in their late 40's-60's depleted, with health problems, feelings of depression, extra weight, and low energy/vitality.

Restoring your vitality starts with a decision to take control of your GPS! The chapters that follow will provide you with habits and actions you can take to look, feel, and perform as if you are a decade younger. You will only be able to take these actions and reap the rewards if you have committed to taking a proactive approach to your life. Are you ready to reprogram your GPS?

How to Create a New Expectation

The first step to experiencing an amazing aging experience is to **expect it** for yourself and **believe** you can have it! The second step is to write it down. In this book you will notice that I often tell you to write out thoughts, intentions, commitments, and changes. There is something truly magical that happens when we externalize our intentions into words, either keyed or penned. Researchers on the human brain have discovered in study after study that writing down your goals and intentions has a HUGE positive impact on your success in making your intentions/dreams/goals become your reality.

Why does writing down your goals and dreams have such a profound impact? The explanation has to do with the way our brains work. As you may know, your brain has a left and a right hemisphere.

The wide, flat bundle of neural fibers that connects the two hemispheres is called the corpus callosum. This is the conduit through which the electrical signals between the right brain, which is imaginative, and the left brain, which is literal, make contact.

These electrical signals then move into the fluid that surrounds the brain and travels up and down the spinal column. Finally, these signals then communicate with every fiber, cell and bone in our body... to the consciousness that operates within us to transform our thoughts into reality.

This is significant because if you just THINK about one of your goals or dreams, you're only using the right hemisphere of your brain, which is your imaginative center.

But, if you think about something that you desire, and then write it down, you also tap into the power of your logic-based left hemisphere!

The act of writing down your dreams and goals integrates both hemispheres of the brain and also ignites a powerful resource you need to make them a reality! This powerful resource is your subconscious mind.

To reiterate, you will be challenged in this book to begin thinking proactively, and then to put your goals and intentions into writing so that you will be successful! Do it, *every time* you are prompted to in this book. I want you to be successful in creating an amazing life experience!

In addition to becoming proactive about your life, another aspect of creating a successful mindset about aging involves eliminating the "age-card". If you have found yourself blaming life circumstances on your age, I challenge you to let go of that excuse! If you are 50 and your knee hurts, do you think "I must be getting old"? Maybe there is an issue with your knee that needs to be addressed, a non-age-related knee problem that anyone could have whether you were 17 or 40 or 80!

If you notice you have lost your flexibility, and think "I can't bend over like I used to" .... does that have anything to do with age?

What if you lost your flexibility because you stopped stretching or challenging your body to move in full range of motion? I have seen this loss of mobility in humans as young as 10 years old! Mobility is lost when it's not used every day, not because you're "getting old"! We will go much further into the topic of mobility in Chapter 3, "Move with Ease," as it is a key component to having a high quality of life as you age.

Maybe you don't get a promotion at work, or you lock your keys in the car, or you forget where you placed your sunglasses. These things happen to people in their 20's and they happen to people in their 60's. Don't allow yourself to blame your age for these every-day occurrences!

My challenge for you is to eliminate the "age card". Do not use your age as an excuse for anything, instead, take responsibility for ways that you may have allowed your strength or mobility or health to decline so that you can be empowered to do something about it! Take responsibility for acquiring the skills you need to get the promotion, or give yourself grace for making a human error, or learn how to create better organizational systems. I realize this may offend some people. We have built reasons in our minds about how our age will limit us. Our culture reinforces the concept by constantly portraying older individuals as weak and physically incapable, so it is easy for this belief to seep into our expectations. If left unchallenged, we accept these expectations about aging as our plight in life.

You can blame many things for the current state of your body. Perhaps genetics (such as having high blood pressure in the family

It might not be your fault, but it is still your responsibility.

history), an injury, or even a medical professional putting a limiting belief in your mind that you accepted about what you "can't" do. There is a long line of things to blame for the current condition of your body. While some causes are out of your control, MANY factors you do have the ability and power to improve. Your body ultimately is an outward reflection of your choices, values, and beliefs. Until you accept responsibility for certain aspects of your physical health, you will not be able to do anything to improve it.

Being younger starts with thinking you can be. Think about what you CAN do and still want to do! Expose the beliefs you have about aging and see if you are comfortable with where those beliefs will lead you. Once you expose what you really have projected or expected yourself to be in 20 years, the next step is to proactively replace that image.

Writing Exercise: Upgrade Your Mindset

First you will need to write (yes with pen and paper) a description of WHO you'd like to be in 20 years, very detailed. How will you look, how will you move, what will you have accomplished, what will you be able to do and experience on a daily basis, what will your lifestyle be like, who will you spend time with? Allocate at least 15 minutes to write in detail how you would like to experience life as an older adult. NOW YOU ARE ACTIVELY RESETTING YOUR INNER GPS! Put this book down now and commit into writing, in detail, how you would like to experience life as a 70, 80, and 90-year-old.

Once you are clear about where you are going, you will need to replace some reactive beliefs you may have held with new and empowering beliefs. You will need to listen to what you say, either out loud in conversations or to yourself. Are you thinking/saying things like "I'm too old for that," or "Just wait till you turn X," or "At my age..."? That language, and more importantly that line of thinking, needs to be consciously changed to more empowering words and thoughts like "I can X" or "I will X". Eliminate the age card. What can or will you do today, tomorrow, and in 20 years? Some examples of empowering beliefs:

"I can be strong and fit the rest of my life."
"I can regain my flexibility."
"I will always work to keep my muscle tissue."
"I will invest my time in activities that make me vibrant."
"Every time I do my mobility work, I move with greater ease."

An important aspect of having a mindset that creates a youthful body is to set goals for yourself. Is there any reason you can't hike a mountain when you're 70? Or learn to salsa dance when you're 80? Or do 60 pushups when you turn 60? Or learn to play piano and have your first recital at any age? I experienced such joy helping a 70-year-old man, who had not exercised in decades, build himself up to 20 pushups on the floor again! He came to my facility at 70 years old and wanted to get back in shape, and he sure did! It started with a belief that it was possible. Set exciting goals for yourself, short term and long term!

Raising Your Standards

A part of creating a mindset that allows you to be youthful is to create standards for your physical capability as you age. For example, maybe a standard is "I will exercise in some fashion every day as long as I live", or "I will never stop using the stairs" or "As long as I can, I will". Standards are powerful! Unfortunately, many of the standards we have for our behavior, we are not even aware of as they are conditioned/programmed on a subconscious level. I heard a healthy man in his early 60's asking for help to move an air conditioner. I knew this man had moved it many times himself, so I asked him why he wanted help. He stopped to consider for a minute and replied "Well, I'm getting older now". He was still physically capable of moving it, but had lowered his expectation for himself because of his age.

Are you looking to buy a single level home so that you will not have to traverse steps as you age? Does that reveal a hidden belief that you expect you will no longer be strong or mobile enough to traverse them? Why not keep your body strong and active so that stairs are not a challenge for you! How about tying your shoelaces? When did you stop kneeling or sitting on the floor to tie them, and why did you choose to sit on a chair? Most people would not know this answer because, when you are on autopilot, your body will always choose the most efficient and easiest means of accomplishing tasks. At one point, as your mobility declined, it became easier to sit in a chair and now that is your habit.

Other "aids" also enable us to decline in physical capacity, such as shoe horns, back scratchers to wash our backs, and slip-on shoes instead of sneakers with laces. What other modifications to your lifestyle have you already adopted that make movement "easier" or decrease the amount of challenge or effort needed? At some point, you lowered your standards/expectations for yourself.

It is not easy to change our culturally programmed standards of aging, so another major key to doing this is to start looking up to people who have the lifestyle and youthfulness you want to experience as you age! I did not even realize it was possible to look and feel great into 70-90's, or to keep achieving great things until I started seeing real-life people doing it. Now I have many role models who have raised my standards!

There are many examples of people who enjoyed a high-quality life, staying fit and active until the end! Consider **Jack LaLanne**, a pioneer of fitness. Jack worked out his whole adult life, 2 hours every day, until the day he died (age 96). He also performed amazing feats of strength in his older age, and his mindset about aging and nutrition was a game-changer. Read "Live Young Forever", his last book. Consider **Harriette Thompson**, a 91-year-old runner who completed her 15th marathon in San Diego just weeks after undergoing radiation treatment. Consider **Hershel McGriff**, who won a NASCAR race at age 61 and still raced into his 80's, coming in 13th in a race at age 81.

I could go on and on listing individuals over 50 years old who will help you raise your standards and reshape your perspective of what a great aging experience can look like. At the end of each chapter in this book I will highlight an older adult who is a great example of living life to the fullest. Also, if you type "Bored Panda: the age of happiness" in your browser you will find a long list of Seniors who will inspire you! These pictures and stories of vibrant seniors include skydivers to DJ's to Magicians to Athletes, all who are living rich, youthful lives into their 80's and 90's. When you surround yourself with people, stories/images of people who have counter-cultural values and thoughts about aging, it will help you to raise your expectations for what your body or health could be like! What your mind may have believed was impossible is replaced with the reality that whatever you decide is possible will be possible!

The last important factor in changing your mindset about aging is to get around people who also want to live a high quality of life and do not make excuses for why they cannot. Think about the stereo-typical social life of an older person. Here's the scene: A table at a local diner with older adults complaining about aches and pains, their most recent trip to the doctor, the cost of their medication, or an upcoming surgery. The focus of such individuals is on factors they can't control, and the belief is that they are victimized by life circumstances (reactive thinking). If you continue to hang out with people who think this way, you WILL become like them. Find friends who are proactive about their lives! Be around people who are setting goals and encouraging you to set yours!

It has been said that we become like the 5 people we spend the most time with, whether we want to be like them or not! Think about the 5 people that you spend the most time with right now... are you comfortable with their values, lifestyle, physique, fitness level, intentionality about life? If not, you need to make some changes. Get around people who are staying fit, setting goals for themselves, living a lifestyle that promotes youth, or who are willing to be challenged and motivated by your desire to have a vibrant life. When you make some changes to your lifestyle and mindset, you can expect that a few people close to you will discourage you, ushering you back into your realm of comfort. They might scoff at your goal to achieve X by age X, or tell you what "reality" is. Be prepared, and also be prepared to spend more time with people who will make you more awesome!

Summary

I started the book with the hardest chapter (and lesson) to accept, but absolutely the most important—changing your mindset. Your inner life dictates your outer life. Do the work inside first, then take on the next several chapters!

Here's a quick summary of what we learned in this chapter and the key takeaways:

1. Expose what you have currently feared/projected yourself to be as an older person, then choose how YOU want to experience life as you age. **WRITE IT DOWN IN DETAIL.**

2. Raise your standards for what you can and will do as you age. Catch your thoughts and language, upgrade to "I will" and "I can".

3. Set goals for yourself. **Put them in writing**, and never stop setting them.

4. Find role models, people who live with vitality and refuse to "be old". Read books by them, post quotes by them or pictures of them on your vision board or refrigerator or screen saver, and follow them on social media.

5. Spend time around other people who are also being proactive about their lives.

Ernestine Shepherd, 77

Ernestine can bench press 150 lbs. and runs an average of 80 miles per week! She didn't start working out until her 50's!

CHAPTER 2:
NUTRITION THAT
PREVENTS AGE

"The food you eat can either be the safest and most powerful form of medicine, or the slowest form of poison"
–Ann Wigmore

The things that you eat have a tremendous impact on your health and well-being over the long term. Health experts have even started to claim that *the entire well-being of an individual can be determined by their gut health.* The only way the nutrients in your food get delivered to your awaiting cells is by being broken down and absorbed in your gut. Your cells need these precious nutrients to repair themselves, grow, and be vibrant. The cells in your body are constantly being damaged, and your body has the ability to repair them when given the right nutrients and environment! However, without a healthy gut to break down and absorb your food, it is possible that the precious nutrients you take in will get passed through you with no benefit, leaving you deficient and malnourished, leaving cells damaged and aging

So, what's the key to a healthy gut?

Bacteria: The Key to Healthy Digestion

"All disease begins in the gut"

–Hippocrates

A healthy gut holds trillions of helpful bacteria, which are critical to our immune system as they protect us from harmful bacteria, and also help our food digest properly. These bacteria even produce vitamins! The human body holds MORE bacterial cells than human cells,[1] so technically we are more bacterial than human!

The study of gut bacteria is a newer frontier in medicine, and scientists are even referring to the trillions of bacteria as an organ! Research is now showing a correlation between poor gut health and disease, including diabetes, mental health, arthritis, heart disease, cancer and obesity. It is your job to be a caretaker to these trillions of friends living inside you! Give them love, and they'll give you life.

The key to high functioning nutrient absorption, as well as overall wellness in the body, is to maintain a healthy gut bacterial balance. How does our helpful/harmful bacterial balance become unhealthy in the first place? Antibiotics, chronic stress, illness, cigarette smoking, lack of life-force foods (whole food) in the diet, and lack of sleep create an unhealthy gut. If you have any of these factors in your life, your gut bacteria is compromised and you are at risk for developing a lifestyle disease.

---

[1] Nicola Davis, "The Human Microbiome: Why our microbes could be the key to our health", *The Guardian*, March 26 2018

Antibiotics kill massive amounts of bacteria in your body, both good and bad. Avoid taking them at all costs, using only as a last resort. In recent years there has been more public education on the damaging effects of antibiotic use, and most doctors now do not prescribe antibiotics as readily. If you have taken antibiotics, it is necessary to take a high concentration of probiotics to replace what was destroyed.

A very recent study on the correlation between sleep and gut bacteria showed that in just 2 nights of sleep deprivation (4 hours of sleep each night), there was already a shift in gut balance that caused an increase in the number of bacteria that promotes diabetes and weight gain![2] Adequate sleep is needed to keep a healthy gut (the topic of sleep is covered in much more detail in Chapter 7.)

Research on gut bacteria and stress is new and fascinating! We have known for a while that chronic stress causes disease. We know it affects your brain, your heart, your metabolism, your libido as well as a slew of other health problems. New research shows us that our gut bacteria is negatively affected by stress!

One way to increase or replace the good bacteria that was lost/ destroyed is to ingest more of them! Fermented drinks such as kombucha, organic yogurts, fermented foods such as kimchi and sauerkraut, miso, apple cider vinegar, and probiotic supplements are some ways in which to do this. Take them daily to build your-

---

[2] Abstract: "Gut microbiota and glucometabolic alterations in response to recurrent partial sleep deprivation in normal-weight young individuals". October 2016

self back up. These foods mentioned are alive, full of life, and in-line with the nutritional anti-aging secret, which I am about to re-veal to you.

The Nutrition Secret That Will Prevent Aging

It is important to remember that the effects of the food you ingest are not always immediate. You might eat a donut and not notice a difference in your health. You may drink 1-2 sodas per day and not feel unhealthy. You might be eating a diet of 50% processed foods and still feel ok. The effects are long term! The good news is that you can start to invest in your body TODAY and reap the benefits for the rest of your life, as your body is constantly making new cells and regenerating itself. To look and feel decades younger, just fol-low this simple nutrition secret: *Eat food that has life in it!*

What does that mean? Any food that is consumed in its purest form, in which it was created, is perfect and full of life. Think of an egg: It contains all the nutrients needed to give life to a chick! There is life force in that egg! Compare that to a cracker. The grain was harvested and dried and stripped of all nutrients, then bleached and churned with other chemicals and ingredients before being salted and packaged with preservatives. Then it may have sat on a shelf for another 6 months. There is no life force in this cracker at all, and a cracker isn't even the worst of the foods I could've picked for comparison!

Life Foods

Any food that comes from a plant and is consumed in its original state is going to be full of life! Think of seeds.... they have so much life force in them that, when planted, they can produce an entire plant/tree! This tree/plant then produces scores of fruit that contain even more seeds! All Fruits and Vegetables have life force in them, as they are picked fresh from the earth and carry seeds with all their powerful life force. Compare a fresh picked strawberry, full of little life-force seeds, nutrients, vitamin C, and fiber, to a low-life fruit, let's say a jar of applesauce from the store. The apples have been boiled, causing nutrients to leach out, then stripped of their skins and fiber, and churned up and mixed with preservatives and often sweeteners. There is barely any life-force left in that jar!

Proteins

Comparing proteins, let's look at the life force in a wild caught Salmon. This healthy animal was fit and active when caught. The only ingredient on the label is SALMON. Compare this to a sausage, which is comprised of the lowest quality parts of a stressed and caged animal, whose cells carry stress hormones. Those low-quality bits have then been processed on machinery and mixed with other agents. There is barely any life-force in the sausage.

Fats

Comparing fats, consider the life-force in an avocado. It contains enough life to create a new tree! It is full of vitamins and antioxidants, and most importantly monounsaturated fat (anti-inflammatory effect). Compare this fat to vegetable oil. This oil is often made from genetically modified seeds that are heavily sprayed with pesticides. They are then processed with harmful chemicals, then the product is bleached and deodorized to hide the rancid smell. The final product is far removed from its life source. Not only does this product fail to deliver nutrients or life to your body, it is actually harmful as many experts are linking vegetables oils to increased risk of heart disease.

Starches

Comparing starches now, consider a sweet potato. It is loaded with fiber and vitamins, pulled right from the earth in the state it was created. It has the power to replicate itself as it would send out shoots and have the life-force to grow more plants if left in the earth. Compare to a piece of bread, with an ingredient list of 10-20 additives, preservatives, even coloring. Even whole grain bread from a shelf, while containing more fiber and traces of protein as the wheat husk has not been bleached or destroyed, still is heavily processed and cannot give life (except to mold lol!).

The simple question to ask when making choices about what you will eat—*if* you are eating to reverse aging—is, "How close is this food to its life source?" Keep track of what you are currently eating, and count how many items you eat daily came directly from a plant or animal that was freshly harvested/butchered/filleted. As an example, if you find that only 20% of your food intake is full of life, the first step would be to set the goal for 50%! Habits take time, so strive for progress, not perfection. The payoff for investing time and money into eating more Life-filled foods (however less convenient at times) is enormous!

Antioxidants

Another reason that food directly from the earth (life force) is so essential to keeping a low body age is because plant foods contain the highest levels of antioxidants. Antioxidants are compounds found in food that protect our cells by stopping or delaying the damage caused by free radicals. Free radicals are unstable molecules that are missing an electron, and when in contact with a healthy cell will steal it from that cell. This weakens and damages the healthy cell, and we age. Antioxidants will sacrifice themselves, allow themselves to be bonded to the free-radical so that it does not damage other healthy cells! Free radicals exist naturally in the body as they are the byproduct of metabolism, and in a healthy body they are kept in check. They get out of balance due to poor nutrition, pollutants in the environment, things we inhale (such as cigarette smoke), chemical additives we ingest through processed foods, and stress.

Mounting evidence indicates the key to slowing aging is increasing antioxidants. One study after another has shown that antioxidants help prevent cancer and heart disease, safeguard memory, reduce the risk of degenerative diseases like Parkinson's and Alzheimer's, protect your joints, soothe pain, reduce muscle soreness and fatigue, avert blindness caused by macular degeneration and cataracts, and even ward off wrinkles.

Your best offense to defeat the free radicals is building up your army of antioxidants through an antioxidant-rich diet!

Less Quantity, Longer Life

A factor related to longevity worth mentioning relates to food quantity. Several research studies have found that people who eat LESS live longer. Many studies suggest 15% less than you are currently eating increases your life span.[3] This is actually quite logical, as those who eat less are dumping fewer amounts of toxins in their bodies, creating less stress on all the systems, and therefore less free-radical production.

Beverages

There are many misleading marketing ploys that leave people confused as to which beverages are healthy. Just for fun, I could take a can of diet soda and label it "Fat Free! Cholesterol Free! Gluten Free! Sugar Free!" and while that information is all true, it is highly misleading as the overall devastation that soda creates in the human body would make that product worthy of a trash can. Marketers will call attention to buzz words we accept as "healthy" to make products sell. Many people are drinking beverages every day that are marketed as "healthy", but that are slowly poisoning their bodies! The priority for a business is revenue, NOT your health as touted on the label. Take responsibility to police what you put in your body.

Again, use the "close to life" rule when choosing beverages. Pure water, bone broth, kombucha, coffee, tea, and pure 100% organic juices are going to bring you life.

---

[3] Susan Scutti, "Cut calories by 15% to stay young, study says", *CNN*, March 22, 2018

Water

Do not drink waters that have been sweetened in any way! Our grocery store shelves are lined with all kinds of waters. Read the labels carefully. Most of them are artificially sweetened with chemicals that are foreign to the human body, indigestible, and do not have enough decades of research to show what harm these toxins may be causing us. There are also various types of plain, unsweetened carbonated water in 3 main categories: seltzer water, sparkling mineral water, or club soda. Sparkling water, or mineral water, is water from a spring that is naturally carbonated and contains natural minerals! This is the best choice for enjoying a "fizz" in your water. Club soda and seltzer waters are artificially carbonated and club soda has sodium added to it. The best choice of beverage is pure water, or sparkling mineral water. If you really need flavor to enjoy water, you can add your own fruit in an infusion pitcher or bottle.

Juices

Juicing, especially at home where ingredients are controlled, is a great way to take in large volumes of antioxidants and other beneficial nutrients. There are many books and resources available that provide recipes and tips about how and why to juice vegetables and fruits if you would like to add fresh juice to your diet. I will not go into more detail here, just introduce you to the concept.

Be careful of any juices or smoothies you buy commercially, as even the ones that say "no added sugar" will generally have 40-70g of natural sugar from all the fruit used to sweeten it. A typical 12oz soda has 40g of sugar, so even though the juice is "healthy" and the sugar is "natural", you are actually drinking almost double the amount of sugar you would have in a soda! Read the nutrition label and list of ingredients. Manufacturers know that a great-tasting product will sell! Also, many times a commercial juice is so high in natural sugar that the manufacturer will split it into 2 servings per bottle so the grams of sugar appear to be lower. Most people drink the whole bottle, not knowing that it is a "double" serving!

If you are buying your juice at a fresh juice bar, it also will contain high amounts of natural sugar from their fresh fruits. The metabolic effect caused by drinking these high sugars outweigh the benefits of the nutrients and antioxidants in these juices. For that reason, juices that are commercially sold or even sold at a local fresh juice stand should be limited to 2 or less per week.

Two beverages surrounded by clouds of conflicting information are alcohol and coffee. I will address the nutrition value of these beverages *only as it relates to a youthful and vibrant body* (and not for any other health reasons).

Alcohol

Red wine contains high levels of antioxidants and one 8oz glass/day or less does promote growth of healthy gut bacteria! If your dietary goals are to support weight loss, sport performance, or for medical reasons, please read information regarding the effect of alcohol on those specific goals, and remember that for the purpose of this book I address alcohol solely for its potential benefits to being youthful! Other alcohols beside red wine actually cause damage to the gut and provide no nutritional value. Other types of alcohol promote inflammation in the body!

Coffee and Tea

Coffee contains several types of antioxidants! Caffeine, whether from tea or coffee, is a performance enhancer and will help you get more out of your workout if consumed prior to exercise. However, the caffeine in coffee does cause calcium to leach from your bones if consuming more than 18oz/day. Decaffeinated coffee is a way to enjoy some of the benefits without the side-effects from caffeine, however, there are slightly less antioxidants in decaf coffee. Enjoy your coffee, in moderation!

Tea, in general, has been used for health benefits for thousands of years! All teas (black, green, white, oolong) contain antioxidants and because tea contains lower levels of caffeine than coffee, you can enjoy 3-5 cups per day and still receive health benefits with no adverse effects. You can enjoy it hot or cold. If you are drinking tea cold, make it yourself. Many commercially-made cold teas are extremely high in sugar, artificial colors, and artificial flavors. These additives cause the tea to be more toxic than helpful!

Kombucha is a drink made from black tea that is full of pro-biotics and antioxidants! People enjoy the taste as it is fizzy and slightly sweet. It contains live cultures of yeast and helpful bacteria. Because it is living and potent, it -shouldn't be consumed more than 6-8 oz per day.

If you cannot drink plain tea (hot nor cold) and must sweeten it, I provide some natural options as follows.

Sweeteners

Follow the *Living Younger* principle of "Eat foods containing Life Force" when looking for ways to sweeten drinks, shakes, or sweet treats. Any sweetener that was made in a lab is unnatural to your body. Not only do these chemicals or processed sugars fail to provide life force, they are actually toxic to your system! **Honey** is a natural product of bees and provides many health benefits. Organic honey that is unprocessed would be full of life force! **Stevia** is extracted from the Stevia plant, and provides a very sweet taste without calories or negative impact on blood sugar levels. Check the label when buying stevia to make sure it does not have other blends of sweeteners added to it! Agave Nectar was originally made in Mexico and because it was derived from the Agave plant, it had medicinal properties. However, those properties have been destroyed in the commercial making of agave syrup, as heat and enzymes are added that remove any health benefits and make the agave nectar to affect your body in the same way as high-fructose corn syrup.

Sugar that is processed commercially in any form (white sugar, corn syrup, and xylitol to name a few) is going to cause stress systemically, and for that reason the less of it you consume, the better you will look and feel.

Soda

No. Just no. I would need several pages to explain the devastating effects soda has on almost every system in your body, with no nutritional return. Equate soda to poison. Every time you drink soda, know that you are damaging, polluting, and aging your beautiful body that works so hard to keep you healthy.

Spices, Herbs, and Supplements

There are entire books devoted to nutrition, that will break down the benefits of all foods, plants, and herbs. These resources will give you extensive details about the healing properties and nutritional values of any food you desire to learn about. For the purposes of this book, I will list some of the most life-giving and beneficial items to add to your diet, but will keep details to a minimum. I invite you to do further research on your own as the following spices, herbs, and supplements will improve the health and function of your body!

Regarding herbs and spices, ALL of them **contain high levels of antioxidants**! Remember this while you are cooking: *the more herbs and natural spices you can add to your food the better your body will be*! Enjoy them fresh or dried, and use them liberally. A few examples of herbs/spices are oregano, parsley, cilantro, basil, cumin, turmeric, and cinnamon.

Bone Broth is a great food to add to your diet! Bone Broth contains high levels of collagen and contains "anti-aging" minerals such as calcium, phosphorus, and magnesium. It also contains **glucosamine, chondroitin and hyaluronic acid,** which improve joint health. Bone broth can be made at home, purchased in liquid form, or purchased in powder form to be dissolved into hot water. Make sure it is organic and made from grass-fed beef!

Turmeric is a spice that gives curry and mustard their yellow coloring. Made from the root/stem of the plant, it has been used medicinally for thousands of years to treat a variety of ailments. It is mostly valued for its use as an anti-inflammatory, comparable to ibuprofen except with no toxic effect to the human body! It is used as an effective and natural treatment for arthritis, digestive issues, and is shown to prevent certain cancers.

Acetyl-L-Carnitine is an honorable mention. While I believe that the best supplements come in whole food form, research is promising on the effects of this supplement on older adults as far as reducing inflammation and creating energy as well as improved cognition. Acetyl-L-Carnitine is produced naturally in your body, but can be taken in supplement form as you age and your body produces less.

Apple Cider Vinegar is widely accepted as a healthy addition to your diet, credited with a host of beneficial effects on your health! It contributes to an improved aging experience as it will keep your gut bacteria healthy and happy.

Probiotic supplements will build up a healthy colony of helpful bacteria, the bacteria that may have been killed off by stress, poor diet, anti-biotics, or overtaken by harmful bacteria.

Vitamin D serves a variety of anti-aging purposes! It is needed to manufacture testosterone, it interacts with calcium to build bone density, and it elevates mood. It is manufactured perfectly in your own body but only in response to sunlight on your skin. If you do not receive more than 20 minutes per day of direct sunlight, a supplement should be considered.

I have listed very few supplements because in general, supplements are not as effective as whole food sources. Firstly, the industry is not regulated by the FDA so you could be buying a capsule of filler or powder (at best)! Secondly, supplements artificially extract parts of plants or animals, taking them away from their natural delivery source and often rendering them unabsorbable. Put the pills down and eat real food! The best delivery source for ANY vitamin or nutrient is in its natural state. Omega 3 is a popular supplement for heart health, however the body best absorbs this fatty acid in the form of fatty fish (mackerel, salmon, herring, oysters, sardines), flaxseeds, and walnuts. Vitamin pills will not replace a poor diet.

Herbs/Supplements for vitality over 40:

Bone Broth

Turmeric

Acetyl-L-Carnitine

Apple Cider Vinegar

Probiotics

Vitamin D

The "Costs" of Eating Healthy

One concern I frequently hear about changing to a diet of fresh plant-based foods and organic meats is the increase in cost. I promise you that spending an extra $50-$100/month to buy life-filled, pure foods is a fraction of what you will pay in medications, surgery, and disease recovery if you do not care for your body now! Also, eliminating expenses like soda, commercial beverages, fast food, and alcohol would easily save that same amount of money per month. The way we spend money is actually a projection of our value system, so check yourself if you are feeling unwilling to spend a little more on the way you fuel your body. What price would you put on feeling, looking, and performing 10 years younger? What price will you pay in 20 years on medications and medical appointments for lifestyle related diseases that are preventable?

Summary

The items that you eat and drink play a major factor in how quickly your body ages! Taking control of what you put into your body is a way to be proactive about creating a great aging experience and also preventing diseases! Making simple swaps like eating an apple instead of a processed granola bar, or buying salmon instead of sausage at the grocery store, are within your control. Don't have a perfectionistic or "all or nothing" mindset about improving your nutrition! Making upgrades to the foods you are eating is a <u>process</u> and over the next few months you can slowly make small changes, learn new recipes, and make different choices at restaurants or the grocery store. It is easy to make small changes that create a great long-term impact.

I understand that it can also be very difficult to upgrade your nutrition if you have developed a psychological or physical addiction to certain foods or eating habits. Foods containing sugar are highly addicting, as well as sodas, energy drinks, and alcohol. If you would like to eliminate these things from your diet, or have tried before and been unsuccessful, you may consider working with a coach briefly, or using an accountability group/partner. There are many effective strategies out there for coaching habit changes!

Here is how to eat in order to create a great aging experience!

1. Eliminate the foods/beverages that could be destroying your helpful gut bacteria.
2. Eat foods that contain life! Foods that were recently picked, harvested, caught, or butchered add life force to your body.
3. Increase foods that contain antioxidants!
4. Eat less.
5. Consider adding supplemental foods that support your digestion, bone health, or joint health.

Foods High in Life Force

PROTEINS:
*Choose Wild caught instead of commercially farmed!
Fish
Grass-fed beef, steak
Wild caught seafood (lobster, shrimp, scallops, crab, mussels)
Free Range Chicken
Wild Duck/ Wild Turkey
Lamb
Deer/elk/bison, any wild game
Eggs from cage free chickens
Organic Greek Yogurt

VEGETABLES:
*All veggies contain life-force! Eat 5-7 per day (based on your bodyweight)!
*Eat fresh or frozen instead of canned
*Eat them raw, steamed, or quickly cooked on high heat rather than boiled to preserve the nutrients

Vegetables with Highest Antioxidants:
Kale/Spinach/Dark greens
Beets
Brussel Sprouts
Broccoli Florets
Red Bell Pepper
Onion
Garlic
Tomatoes
Purple Cauliflower
Boiled red cabbage
Boiled artichoke
Seaweeds, all varieties

FRUITS:
*All fruits contain life force! Eat 1-3 per day (based on your body-weight)!
*Buy local when in season
*Buy organic if eating the skin of the fruit
*Wash thoroughly
*Eat whole, fresh fruits (not canned, jarred, or preserved)

Fruits with highest antioxidants:
Berries of all kinds
Dark grapes (purple, red, blue)
Cherries
Plums/prunes
Oranges
Mangoes
Figs
Pomegranates

STARCHES:

Root vegetables
Quinoa
Wild Rice
Oats

Starches with Highest Antioxidants:

Beans
Squash
Pumpkin
Potatoes
Sweet potato/yams

FATS:

Real butter
All-natural nut butters (almond, cashew, peanut)

Fats with Highest Antioxidants:

Coconut Oil
Olive Oil
Walnuts, hazelnuts, brazil nuts, pecans, pistachios, almonds
Seeds of all types (chia, flax, sunflower, pumpkin, etc.)
Avocados

BEVERAGES:

Pure Water or Mineral Water
Bone Broth

Highest in Antioxidants:

Green Tea

Kombucha

Red Wine

Coffee

Other Foods High in Antioxidants:

All herbs and spices-Use liberally

Honey

Apple Cider Vinegar

Miso

Cocoa/Dark chocolate

Sauerkraut

Kimchi

Ida Keelig, 102

Ida Keeling set the record as the first 100-year-old person to run the 100m dash, she's 103 now and still running! She also still does her pushups on the floor. She didn't start running until 67 years old! She authored the book "Can't Nothing Bring Me Down".

CHAPTER 3:
MOVE WITH EASE

"Age is no barrier. It's a limitation you put on your mind."
–Jackie Joyner-Kersee

The ability to move easily and in full range of motion allows you to live life to the fullest! When you have good mobility, you can easily hinge, bend, rotate, reach, squat, and lunge! You can effortlessly perform daily activities like bending down to tie a shoe, reaching behind your head to wash your back, sitting cross-legged on the floor, or squatting down to look under the couch for the wayward remote control. Mobility gives you freedom! When you are moving with ease you can enjoy recreational activities such as hunting, sports, hiking, dancing and adventures that require physical exertion. When you lose mobility, these activities become difficult or painful.

Understanding Mobility

Mobility is NOT the same thing as flexibility. Mobility refers to how one MOVES, while flexibility refers to the length of a muscle. Having good flexibility is one of several factors that create mobility. Your goal is to increase overall MOBILITY, as mobility is a greater indicator of longevity and quality of life.

Losing your mobility is not a direct result of aging! Note that in the picture below, this elderly gentleman can sit comfortably on his haunches with no loss of mobility in ankle, knee, or hip. If you observe children under the age of 5, they play comfortably in this position! By the age of 20, most Americans are unable to sit this way. Take a minute to get into this position and see how comfortable (or not) it is for you.

Much of mobility loss has to do with our constant sitting in chairs. From age 5, we sit on a chair for breakfast, sit on a school bus bench, sit on a chair at a desk for 6 hours at least, sit on the bus home, sit to do homework, sit to eat dinner, sit to watch TV. Our body is locked in the same position for hours each day. Over several years, muscles in our legs/hips/ankles shorten and we are no longer able to comfortably sit in a deep squat position. The good news is that since we trained our bodies over time to adapt to a seated chair position, we can train our bodies over time to regain their full range of motion! In this chapter you will learn how your joints, your level of flexibility, and your muscle fascia all work together to create mobility. I will also show you how to improve your current level of mobility!

Mobility and Correlation to Longevity

In addition to making us feel young, our ability to move with ease is directly related to how long we will live. A few years ago, a study by

Brazilian doctor and longevity expert Claudio Gil Araujo was published in American and European medical journals. He and his team of Brazilian researchers developed a deceptively simple measure of musculoskeletal fitness which can predict who will live longer and whose lives will be cut short.

This test is a variation on the classic chair test (where a subject is asked to stand up from a seated position in a chair), which doctors have long used to assess leg strength and lower body fitness in seniors. This newer sit-down-stand-up test was designed to provide a window into a person's ability to function well and remain autonomous. It calls for flexibility, balance, motor coordination, and, most importantly, ample muscle power relative to body weight.

In the study, 2002 men and women ages 51 to 80 were followed for an average of 6.3 years, and those who needed to use both hands and knees to get up and down (whether they were middle-aged or elderly) were almost seven times more likely to die within six years than those who could spring up and down without support.[4] Their musculoskeletal fitness, as measured by the test, was lacking. And musculoskeletal fitness, it turns out, is very important. If you would like to try the test, follow the instructions below[5] (Illustration by Roen Kelly, Discovermagazine.com).

---

[4] Araujo, C.G., and others, "Ability to sit and rise from the floor as a predictor of all-cause mortality" *NCBI* abstract, December 13, 2012
.https://www.ncbi.nlm.nih.gov/pubmed/23242910

[5] Bee Wilson, "Simple Sitting Test Predicts How Long You'll Live", *Discover Magazine*, November 2013.

1. Stand in comfortable clothes in your bare feet, with clear space around you.
2. Without leaning on anything, lower yourself to a sitting position on the floor.
3. Now stand back up, trying not to use your hands, knees, forearms or sides of your legs.

Hand: 1 point | Knee: 1 point | Forearm: 1 point | One hand on knee or thigh: 1 point | Side of the leg: 1 point

Scoring:

The two basic movements in the sitting-rising test — lowering to the floor and standing back up — are each scored on a 1-to-5 scale, with one point subtracted each time a hand or knee is used for support and 0.5 points subtracted for loss of balance; this yields a simple 10-point scale.

Healthy Joints

To enjoy a high degree of mobility, healthy joints are needed! While the human body has several types of joints, the focus in this chapter is on synovial joints. Synovial joints are the joints designed for movement and are made up of bone, cartilage, synovial fluid, ligaments, and muscle.

Synovial fluid is a joint's magic potion. It is an egg-white like substance that exists in your joints. The principal role of synovial fluid is to reduce friction in the joints during movement. It also helps feed and detoxify your joints; it delivers nutrients to the cartilage and removes waste from the cartilage. MOVEMENT is essential for joint health, as movement increases the amount of this precious synovial fluid and pushes the fluid through the joint. Motion is Lotion! While any movement is better than none, the best movements to keep healthy joints are ones that take a joint through its full range of motion! The more variety in movement you get in each joint, the better. The best way to get this "motion lotion" is with very gentle, slow, non-forced movement to your current end-range of motion in each joint.

Nutrition also plays a key role in keeping healthy joints. Plant based foods in general DECREASE inflammation. You can further ensure healthy joints by avoiding certain foods proven to increase inflammation. The foods that trigger the most inflammation are sugar, alcohol, omega 6 fats (such as corn, vegetable, peanut oils) and gluten (a protein in wheat).

Many older adults experience arthritis, a condition of painful inflammation and stiffness in joints. Reducing inflammation through your nutrition (both what you ADD to your diet and what you SUBTRACT from your diet) and a few helpful supplements will help prevent the development of arthritis. If you have already developed arthritis, these nutrition changes will greatly reduce the symptoms you are experiencing.

Supplementation with **glucosamine** (a building block of cartilage), **chondroitin sulfate** (draws water and nutrients to cartilage), **Vitamin D**, and **omega 3 fatty acids** found in oily fish (which reduce inflammation) have been shown to improve joint health. Curcumin, an ingredient in the spice **Turmeric**, can also be taken as a natural anti-inflammatory for joints. Type II Collagen, which can be found in beef bone broth, has also shown significant improvement in joint health. [6] If you are going to add any of these items to your diet, use the fountain of life principle and consume them in their natural state! Increase your levels of Vitamin D from getting 20 minutes of sun if possible, get your Omega 3 from wild-caught, organic fish (free of metals and toxins), add real Turmeric to your foods/teas, and drink bone both daily as it contains collagen, glucosamine, AND chondroitin sulfate.

While improving your nutrition is one of the most important actions you can take to prevent or reduce the symptoms of arthritis, there are some additional lifestyle factors you can control to ensure healthy joints.

Firstly, maintain a healthy body weight. Extra weight was believed to degenerate joints because of the unnatural loading to the joints, but more recent research has shown that the load itself is not as

---

[6] Bagchi D, Misner B, Bagchi M, Kothari SC, Downs BW, Fafard RD, Preuss HG. "Effects of orally administered undenatured type II collagen against arthritic inflammatory diseases: a mechanistic exploration", *NCBI*, 2002

damaging to the joint as the metabolic changes caused by excess fat cells. In studying the correlation between Metabolic Syndrome and inflammation, it is proven that "fat cells pump out inflammation". [7] The joint degenerates more from the toxic environment than from the extra weight load.

Secondly, you can protect your joints by strengthening the muscles around them! Muscles absorb shock and stress, thereby taking wear and tear off your joints. The muscles around your joints provide stability. This is a critical to keeping a joint healthy over time! Having joint stability means that your joint surfaces stay in alignment and that excess motion, outside of a joint's normal range, is prohibited. When you do not have joint stability, the joint surfaces (the ends of your bones) crash into each other during movement and rapidly deteriorate the joint. Joint instability has a high correlation to the development of osteoarthritis![8] Regular strength training exercises will build joint stability and build up the muscles surrounding the joint.

One additional step you can take to keep your joints happy and healthy is to stay hydrated! The cartilage in your joints is made up of 70-80% water. The job of cartilage, such as the meniscus in your knee, is to pad and cushion the joint so the leg bones can move

---

[7] Marion Hauser, "The evidence that abdominal obesity, hypertension, and diabetes is destroying your joints and will send you to a nursing home", *Caring Medical*, Accessed March 2019.

[8] Blalock, Darryl, et al. "Joint Instability and Osteoarthritis." Clinical Medicine Insights. Arthritis and Musculoskeletal Disorders, Libertas Academica, 19 Feb. 2015.

smoothly past one another without grinding. If the cartilage is dehydrated, it becomes more rigid and loses its ability to give the joint a smooth, flexible glide. This creates friction in the joint and leads to cartilage damage. Think of the cartilage as a sponge: when it is dried out it is rough and inflexible, when it is wet is it smooth and pliable.

In summary, you can keep your joints healthy by:

1. Gently moving them to full range of motion (daily)
2. Tweaking your diet to eliminate inflammatory foods
3. Taking some key supplements (whole food form)
4. Keeping a lower bodyweight
5. Staying hydrated!

Flexibility

The length of the muscles that cross through joints determines your level of flexibility (the extent to which you can bend without breaking). Flexibility plays a factor in how mobile you can be! If a muscle shortens over time it will restrict the range of motion in the joint to which it's connected. It is possible to have different levels of flexibility in different body parts! For example, you could have great flexibility in your upper body muscles and poor flexibility in your hamstrings.

Traditional stretching, or static stretching, is not the most effective way to improve flexibility. Historically we believed that a pose should be held for 30-60sec at a certain level of discomfort. In recent years we have found more effective ways of training a muscle to lengthen. Firstly, a muscle should never be stretched to the point of pain or discomfort. This intensity level will activate a protection response in the muscle that will prevent it from lengthening. Stretching must be in a gentle zone!

Secondly, we have found that other forms of stretching are more effective than static hold stretches. PNF stretching (Proprioceptive Neuromuscular Facilitation) seems to produce the best results. This can be done with a partner, with a towel, or another static aid like a doorframe. For PNF stretching, a muscle is taken into a slight stretch for 15 seconds, then the muscle is contracted as you push against a person/towel/prop, holding that contraction for 6-10 seconds before releasing. Another form of stretching that shows better results for improving flexibility is dynamic stretching. This involves moving a muscle through a challenging (but still comfortable) range of motion 10-15 times in a controlled, smooth fashion. A good mobility routine will have several types of dynamic stretches built into it. We will cover this more in Chapter 8!

Muscle Fascia

Another way you can increase your mobility is to decrease any tension held in the muscle or, more importantly, the muscle fascia that overlays and connects major muscle groups. You will not be able to create more flexibility in a muscle that is covered in tight fascia nor increase your range of motion in a joint wrapped in tight fascia!

Fascia is fascinating! Muscle fascia is a sheet or band of connective tissue (mostly made of collagen) laying under the skin that is similar to saran wrap or a spider web. Fascia is very densely woven, covering and interpenetrating every muscle, bone, nerve, artery, and vein in your body. It also covers all of your internal organs including the heart, lungs, brain, and spinal cord.

An interesting aspect of the fascial system is that is it not just a series of separate coverings, it is actually *one continuous structure* that exists from head to toe without interruption. Every part of the entire body is connected to every other part by the fascia, like the yarn in a sweater. Muscle fascia can be damaged and can develop scarring, knots, and it also can become tense when effected by stress. It also holds emotional energy and memory! Sometimes the pain or distress we think we feel in a muscle is actually an injury to the fascia surrounding it, not the muscle itself. I imagine my muscle fascia to be like a stretchy superhero bodysuit that lies just underneath my skin! When I do my mobility work, I imagine the suit stretching and lengthening over top of my muscles. This visual tool helps me to realize the greater impact the movements are having on making my whole body more pliable!

Many times, your **mobility is restricted by tight and tense fascia** and *not* by your muscles being short, inflexible or "tight". "Morning Stiffness" is now believed to be primarily the result of sticky, dehydrated fascia. When you watch a cat or dog wake up, the first thing they do is a full body stretch, which lengthens the fascia in their bodies. If you find yourself stiff in the morning, start out right away with a few minutes of gentle full body stretching and yawning.

Another interesting fact to note about fascia is that since it is one continuous sheet, distress or tightness in one section may create pain or dysfunction in another section. For example, relief from carpal tunnel can be found by releasing the fascia in the Lats (large muscle group running down both sides of the mid back) and upper back. Relief from a "tight IT band" (band of connective tissue running down the outside of the leg from hip to knee) can be found by also relieving tension in the mid-back (Thoracic Spine).

The study of muscle fascia is a newly developing field, and you will hear more and more about this amazing system in the years to come! For the purposes of improving your mobility, just know that it is going to be important for you to give care to your fascia! Caring for your muscle fascia is done in the following ways: yoga, foam rolling, massage, incorporating a variety of movement patterns into your day (mobility routine), and staying hydrated.

Massage and other body work techniques are extremely effective in releasing muscle fascia, however not always practical and affordable. A great alternative is to roll the body several times per week on a foam roller! These firm foam rollers press up against your muscles/fascia as your bodyweight presses down onto the roller. There are many resources online that will teach you how to use the foam roller for all the major muscle groups. In addition to creating healthier fascia, other benefits of regular foam rolling are increased blood flow, increased range of motion and injury prevention. A great resource for video instructions on how to foam roll is the website Stack.com. Search for the article entitled "Foam Rolling Techniques to Fix Every Trouble Spot on Your Body" and you will find a library of videos to teach you how to roll the muscles in each part of your body.

Practice a Mobility Routine

We have amazing bodies that respond to stimuli and can change/ adapt! You CAN regain your mobility! Adding a short mobility routine **every day** as part of your wake-up or going to sleep ritual will restore your ease of movement! The older you are when you start practicing mobility, the more frequent the exposure will need to be. This means you may want to do a few of the exercises 2-3x/day at first if you are serious about regaining your mobility! In Chapter 8, I will give you several examples of simple mobility exercises you could put together into a short mobility routine.

I personally use a mobility routine as the warm up to every strength training session that I do. It prepares my body for the upcoming workout by releasing tension, increasing range of motion for injury prevention purposes, and warming/stretching my muscle fascia. One added benefit I have received simply by adding this pre-workout mobility routine is an increase in my flexibility. My teenage children cannot touch their toes, and this was my plight as well for most of my life until I began doing mobility work. I never practiced touching my toes, nor did stretching routines or prolonged stretching holds, yet a year after I added this mobility routine 3x/week I was able to touch the floor.

Many cultures already have an exercise discipline upheld in their lifestyles that incorporates balance, mobility, and breathwork such as Chinese practices of Tai Chi or Qigong, and Indian practices of Yoga. These are now offered in local gyms/community centers in the U.S. and can be a good resource to take a class for several months. A good instructor will teach you how to get into different positions that will enhance your mobility! These classes improve joint health as they lead you through gentle, slow movements to the end range of a joint's mobility, and also help to release muscle/fascia tension.

Even if you decide not to take a class or practice with a group, **commit to take 5 minutes per day to do your mobility work.** Be excited for it! Be empowered to invest those 5 minutes/day, knowing you will restore the mobility of your youth AND keep your freedom to enjoy all of the physical activities you love!

Take a Stand

There is one small change you could make today that would majorly preserve your mobility, and that would be reduce the amount of time you spend sitting! Sitting in a chair not only deteriorates your muscular-skeletal system, but shortens the quality and quantity of your life! As Americans, we have built our society around chairs, from infancy through end of life. We have special chairs for every age, size, and function. In any business or institution in this country you will find chairs. An American with an office job sits for most of the day! After we sit at work for 5-7 hours, we sit during our commute home, then sit for dinner, then sit for TV/Computer time at home. Sometimes we even sit at the gym! First, you must realize that this amount of sitting in chairs is not normal outside of American lifestyle. People in other cultural lifestyles spend hours of their daily life squatting, sitting on the ground/floor to eat, lounging in a full body stretch for leisure time, standing, and walking for errands or commutes to work. In Lancaster County where I reside, members of the Amish community still walk 1-2 miles to a neighboring farm for a visit or errand.

As research has come out in the last decade, we are finding that the cumulative hours of chair sitting, locked in the same position, are detrimental and unnatural to the human body! Physical Therapists have discovered a root cause of back pain, neck pain, and most hip dysfunction stems from prolonged sitting in chairs. Cardiologists are discovering that a higher risk to heart health, even more than smoking, is extensive sitting. Doctors are linking metabolic diseases such as diabetes and reduced insulin sensitivity to prolonged sitting.

I do want to make you aware of how detrimental chair sitting is to your health and body, and that prolonged sitting will greatly restrict the amount of mobility you will be able to enjoy in your latter years. I'd also like to point you to further research if you're interested in learning more. Two books to consider are "Designed to Move" by Dr. Joan Vernikos (former director of NASA's Life Science Division) and "Get Up: Why your chair is killing you and what you can do about it" by James A Levine, MD.

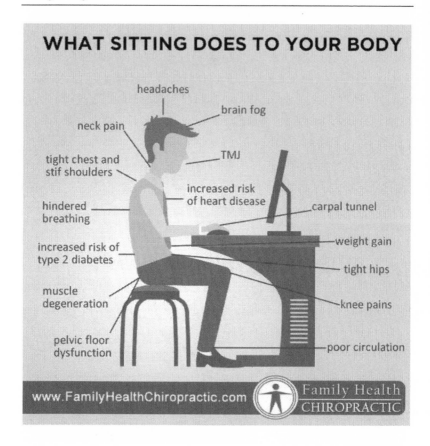

WHAT SITTING DOES TO YOUR BODY

headaches

brain fog

neck pain

tight chest and stif shoulders

TMJ

increased risk of heart disease

hindered breathing

carpal tunnel

increased risk of type 2 diabetes

weight gain

tight hips

muscle degeneration

knee pains

pelvic floor dysfunction

poor circulation

www.FamilyHealthChiropractic.com

Family Health CHIROPRACTIC

You can do something to reduce your "sitting time" starting today! Make it a goal to stand at events whenever you can, stand or sit on the floor when using your computer, lounge on the couch with legs outstretched, or lounge on the carpet/bed for leisure time. Working on the floor will require you to switch positions often. It will also get your joints, particularly hips and knees, in much deeper range of motion than the range they are locked into while sitting on a chair. Standing desks at work or home are a great upgrade! Getting up and down from the floor several times a day, while it may be tedious at first if you haven't been doing this for several years, will eventually get easier and will drastically increase your quality of life! If you have an office job, set a timer to go off every hour while you're at work. When it goes off, that is your reminder to get up and move or do a few mobility exercises for 3-5 minutes. Protect your youthful muscular-skeletal system by sitting in a chair AS LITTLE AS POSSIBLE!

Mobilize, Don't Compromise

The truth is that if we have not maintained our mobility over the years, we will lose it. Many people begin to compensate for their loss of mobility by using aids or lifestyle modifications. These compensations create **even more** loss of mobility! A few examples of lifestyle modifications are wearing slip-on or Velcro shoes to avoid bending/tying, using a shoe horn, bending over at the waist to pick things up instead of lowering into the legs, or using a tool to wash the back in the shower. The market for lifestyle modification products continues to grow as manufacturers see the opportunity to make daily life easier for people with limited mobility.

If we use these products, they allow us to move with even LESS range of motion! Yes, it's easier and less painful to use tools or modifications initially, but long term we are enabling a more rapid decline in our ability to move! If you find there is pain or difficulty reaching behind your head to wash your back, let that be a cue to you that your body is asking for some attention and care for the shoulder/upper back, and lats (latissimus dorsi)! Take the time to foam roll, stretch, and strengthen these areas so that you can not only wash your back, but regain freedom to do several other activities that might involve overhead reaching! Your movement is your freedom!

In addition to using aids/devices to help us do activities, we might start making lifestyle changes that involve less movement. For example, if you are experiencing knee or hip pain, you might take the elevator instead of the stairs to avoid the pain. You might stop sitting on the floor because it hurts to get up. You might stop playing your favorite sport or recreational hobby because the activity causes pain. **PAIN IS A POSITIVE SIGNAL**! Pain is a communication method your body uses to bring attention to **a need for care and nurture**. If your body is sending you pain signals, please choose to address them with attention, care and nurture rather than choose lifestyle modifications that enable you to avoid the signal! Pay attention to your body and its communication to you! If playing basketball or tennis hurts your knees, listen to your body's signal. What if you suspend playing for a few months while you respond to the pain signal by focusing on hydration, changing your diet, strengthening your knee muscles, increasing your mobility, and maybe even consulting a physical therapist? Create an environment where healing can happen, then go back and enjoy your activity!

I hope that after reading this book you will invest your time and money on restoring your mobility instead of buying lifestyle modification products or avoiding the activities that you love!

How to Improve Your Mobility

I want you to be able to move with ease and have a life full of the activities and adventures you love! You do not have to become old, stiff or immobile! I hope that after reading this chapter you believe that you can restore your mobility (if you've lost some already) and feel excited to do so! Here is a summary of some small actions you can take:

1. Commit to a mobility routine at least 1x/day, for a total of 10 minutes* (or a class/group practice)
2. Stay hydrated (your urine should always be pale)
3. Eliminate inflammatory foods
4. Supplement your diet with foods that support joint health
5. Maintain a healthy bodyweight
6. Use foam rolling or massage to release your muscle fascia
7. Sit less
8. Listen to pain signals and address them rather than choose compensatory devices/activities

Let's now explore how your bones and muscles contribute to your ability to move well and learn what you CAN do to keep your body moving well for years to come!

Tao Porchon-Lynch, 95

She's a 96-year-old yoga master (and the world's oldest yoga teacher) as well as the author of several books.

CHAPTER 4:
A YOUNG FRAME

After understanding the importance of mobility, we will now take a look at two major structures in your musculoskeletal system that allow all your glorious movement to happen! Strong bones and strong muscles play a crucial role in preventing age-related physical decline.

Young Bones

Bones aren't sexy. They are functional. Your skeletal system gives you the framework upon which all movement happens. Bones go relatively unnoticed and underappreciated until one breaks!

Fear of falling is common among the elderly, as breaking a bone in older age can cause devastating setbacks and further movement limitations. Many of us know individuals who broke a bone in older age, and thus began a downward slope to other complications or limitations in quality of life. Therefore, it is critical to do what you can to build strong bones!

How to Preserve Bone Density

It is known in the medical community that most of your bone density is gained by the age of 25, and if not maintained, will slowly begin to lose density after that! However, research shows us that it is possible to regain bone density no matter what age, with correct exercises and some key nutrients.[9] One example: A 2016 BMC Musculoskeletal Disorders study of 150 women with osteoporosis or osteopenia found that those who performed regular resistance training increased their serum concentrations of CTX, a marker of bone resorption and formation.[10]

Calcium and Vitamin D are required to form bone density! These vitamins by themselves are not very effective, but when combined with strength training have been proven to increase bone density. Get your calcium from natural food sources and your Vitamin D from the sun! Also, caffeine (more than 18 oz./day), alcohol (more than 1 serving per day), any type of soda, and high levels of dietary sodium cause calcium to leach out of bones. Eating or drinking these items will erode and weaken your bones.

The best exercises for bone health involve applying forces to the bone that send signals to the body to increase bone density! The bone responds to stress/load by becoming thicker and stronger. The two best exercises for keeping bones young and healthy are: 1) Plyometrics (jumping, leaping, skipping, jumping rope, sprinting), and 2) Lifting heavy weights.

---

[9] Senderovich, Helen, et al. "The Role of Exercises in Osteoporotic Fracture Prevention and Current Care Gaps. Where Are We Now? Recent Updates." Rambam Maimonides Medical Journal, Rambam Health Care Campus, 31 July 2017.

[10] Gabriella Császárné Gombos, et al. "Direct Effects of Physical Training on Markers of Bone Metabolism and Serum Sclerostin Concentrations in Older Adults with Low Bone Mass." BMC Musculoskeletal Disorders, BioMed Central, 8 June 2016.

External loads at 1/10 of the force it would take to break a bone are the most effective (termed "minimal essential strain")! Loads must be heavy, with forces greater than you encounter in daily life. A great guideline is that the item (barbell, dumbbell, kettlebell, etc.) must be heavy enough that you simply cannot lift it more than 6-8 times. Ladies, if you grab a 5lb dumbbell and pump it up and down 20x, there will be no change to bone density!

We will cover exercise in more detail in Chapter 8, but be aware that popular exercises such as swimming, biking, and elliptical machines have no positive effect on bone density as they are non-impact activities.

Covet Your Muscle

Building and maintaining muscle is **VITAL** *to having an amazing aging experience!* Muscle is best stimulated through strength training, which is by far the single best form of exercise any adult should be doing for the purposes of enjoying youth and vitality. I want you to understand four major ways that muscle will help you look, function, and feel younger:

1. Muscle gives you Strength
2. Muscle Tissue Improves Hormone Profile
3. Muscle Improves sexual performance
4. Muscle Enhances Physique

Muscle and Strength

Muscular Strength enables you to perform high level activities and sports as you age. Even more importantly, your strength enables you to do daily activities with ease, such as lifting heavy boxes, opening jars, shoveling, bringing in groceries, and getting up from the floor easily. If strength is lost, these daily activities that create independence and a high life quality will become more difficult and eventually you will be unable to do them without help. Keeping your strength, even improving your strength, is needed in order for you to live a high-quality life as you age!

Strength is gained anytime your muscle repeatedly encounters a strain it has not been challenged with before. The muscle responds to the strain by recruiting more muscle fibers, so the adaptation is both muscular AND neurological. The best rep range for building strength is 3-8, so any load that causes strain within this range counts as a strong enough strain to elicit a strength response. The load can come externally (holding objects) or from your own body-weight. For example, if you can barely do 5 pushups on the floor, you are moving a load (your body) in a 3-8 rep range that will elicit a strength response. If you are using objects such as dumbbells or barbells, *they must be heavier than weight you encounter in every-day life.* I've seen ladies at the gym lifting dumbbells that weigh less than their gym bags! This light load will not signal the muscle to become stronger. If a load is light enough to lift/move more than 10x, you are no longer eliciting a true strength response from that muscle.

If you are over 50 years old and have not been strength training, you should be strength training 3x/week as the body will need more stimulus. If you are younger than 50, it is possible to gain strength with 2 lifting sessions per week.

Research in the 1980's opened our eyes to the relationship between strength and quality of life. Testers used a grip-strength test to evaluate one's overall level of strength and found consistently that strength directly correlated to one's quality of life and longevity. Since this discovery, the grip-strength test has become a reliable proxy measure of functional, total-body strength and vitality.

Another study in 2015 in *The Lancet* looked at populations across 17 countries and found that those with the highest grip strength were more likely to live longer. Researchers found that **every 11-pound decline in grip strength** was linked to a 16% increase in death.[11] Low grip strength relative to bodyweight consistently proved to be a predictor of disease, co-morbidity, and disability.[12] The point of this research is not to go out and improve one's forearm strength to live longer, as the strength in the grip is about one's ability to activate many muscles together, including the CNS (central nervous system), to produce force. The way to score better in the test (and increase quality of life) is to bring up your overall level of strength. Hanging and Carrying are two high quality exercises that create total body strength as these exercises actively engage multiple systems. (See Chapter 8 for more on this.)

One concern I have heard from women is a fear of gaining muscle bulk as a result of strength training. Women will not gain muscle bulk on a strength routine done in low rep ranges! For a woman to gain muscle bulk she would need to eat a surplus of food, lift in an

---

[11]"Prognostic value of grip strength: findings from the Prospective Urban Rural Epidemiology (PURE) study", *The Lancet*, Volume 386, Issue 9990, P266-273, July 18, 2015.

[12] Larry Husten, "Get A Grip! Global Study Shows Grip Strength Is A Simple And Powerful Predictor Of Death", *Forbes.com*, May 14, 2015

8-12 rep range 4x/week, and have higher testosterone levels. When strength training in a range of 3-8 reps you WILL gain tone, contour, and firmness in your body along with strength, but not bulk!

Muscle and Hormone Profile

Your muscle not only enables you to be strong enough to do things you want to do as you get older, it also is a metabolically active tissue that secretes proteins! Muscle Tissue could even be considered an endocrine organ because of the effects these secreted proteins (called myokines) have on your hormones. When muscle tissue is stimulated through strength training, it causes the pituitary gland to release "fountain of youth hormones" such as Testosterone and HGH (human growth hormone).

Human growth hormone is a valuable hormone made in the pituitary gland that has been nicknamed the "Fountain of Youth" hormone. It peaks in our teen years, then starts declining in our late 20's. It's responsible for burning fat, regulating blood sugar levels by its effect on insulin, increasing growth of muscle tissue and collagen as well as promoting testosterone. HGH is not safe to take as a supplement and is banned by the World Anti-Doping Agency. There is not enough research to show its effect on the human body over time, and there already several know harmful side-effects. The way to boost your body's production of HGH it is through your lifestyle choices! Deep sleep, intense exercise (including strength training at heavy weight/low reps), and intermittent fasting are the three most proven ways to increase HGH.

Testosterone is a steroid hormone that has beneficial effects for both men and women. It's considered the daddy of all hormones and has many important functions like regulating libido, energy, bone health, immune function and muscular development. Women need this hormone just as much as men do! Women carry significantly lower levels of testosterone in their systems, however it still produces the above benefits. Many of the side effects of aging we dread are related to a decline in testosterone as we age. Testosterone production can be further decreased by high levels of stress, as cortisol will block testosterone production. In both men and women, low levels of testosterone cause loss in muscle strength/mass, increased body fat, fragile bones, low sex drive, insomnia, and lethargy. The good news is that you can naturally increase your body's production of this valuable hormone by strength training! Please read on!

Muscle and Sexual Performance

As we age, we have hidden fears about whether or not we will still be able to perform sexually, and whether we will still be able to have a healthy sex life. Exercise that recruits large amounts of muscle tissue (strength training) is the #1 most effective sexual enhancement treatment. Muscle tissue responds to strength training with the release of the hormones needed to keep your libido high! Strength training will improve your blood circulation, which is vital to sexual performance, and will also give you physical stamina.

There are manufacturers making millions of dollars from selling sexual performance drugs, mostly sold to men. However, there are known negative side-effects to these drugs. While they may increase libido and improve erections, these drugs do not increase the stamina, strength, mobility, or circulation needed to fully enjoy your sex life. No pill can give you sexual vitality the way your own body can when you give it the right tools!

Here are the actions you can take to keep or **improve sexual vitality** as you age:

1. Increase your intake of Vitamin D and Zinc. These are two vitamins found to positively correlate to an increase in testosterone, which increases libido in both men and women. Vitamin D should be increased by exposure to sunlight. The following foods have been shown to aid directly or indirectly in the production of testosterone (also notice how these are already on the *Living Younger* food list for being "full of life" and/or high in antioxidants)

FOODS AIDING IN TESTOSTERONE PRODUCTION

- Pomegranates
- Bananas
- Watermelon
- Coconut/coconut oil
- Avocados
- Oysters
- Tuna
- Garlic
- Honey
- Spinach
- Milk
- Eggs (egg yolk)
- Almonds, pistachios, cashews

---

2. **Get deep sleep.** Testosterone, as well as HGH, is produced in the deep stage of sleep. Sleep deprivation, under 6 hours, has been proven to reduce the body's ability to produce it.

3. **Have sex.** Sexual arousal by itself increases testosterone levels, but the increase in testosterone is substantially greater if one actively participates in sexual activity.

4. **Decrease stress.** This factor will come up again in other chapters as stress has other negative effects on the body and spirit and accelerates the aging process. Stress causes the body to produce cortisol, which steals valuable building blocks needed to produce testosterone. The body treats stress as an emergency, and testosterone as a luxury, so it will give the energy to building cortisol instead of testosterone.

5. **Train your muscles several times per week!** When strength training, use large muscle groups such as glutes, lats, and quads as opposed to smaller muscles like biceps, triceps, and calves.

6. **Get in the sun.** Vitamin D is a major player in the production of testosterone, and our skin produces the majority of our vitamin D by being in direct sunlight.

Muscle and Physique

Your muscle tissue is your biggest asset to having a younger looking physique! Muscle tissue makes you look youthful by giving your body tone and shape, filling out the skin, creating contours, and burning fat. Muscle is sexy at any age! Let's talk about your glutes as an example. They are the largest muscle group in your lower body and create a lovely roundness to your butt. Many elderly people have the trademark of flat, sagging gluteal muscles. This is not a consequence of aging that you must settle for! This is a consequence of allowing that beautiful muscle tissue to atrophy. Strength training the gluteal muscles allows you to enjoy a great looking butt as you age!

Not only does muscle look great on your body, if you train it correctly it will enhance your physique by improving your posture. You will be able to carry yourself high with a strong and straight back. One of the trademarks of elderly people is stooped posture, a forward head, and rounded shoulders. Train your upper back muscles to be strong so that you can carry yourself like you are in your 20's! Strong postural muscles will help you maintain a youthful stature.

Another way that keeping muscle tissue benefits your physique is that it will help you keep a lower body fat percentage. Muscle increases your metabolism, as it is a costly tissue (energy wise) for the body to maintain. This means that muscle tissue burns more energy than other tissues in the body.

While this book promotes youth through balanced care of the mind, body, and spirit, if I had to pick only ONE thing you could do with the biggest return on investment to prevent aging, it would be to KEEP YOUR PRECIOUS MUSCLE TISSUE! So many of the other functions and systems are enhanced/improved by regularly training your muscles.

Summary

Strong bones and strong muscles create the framework for enjoying movement. The byproducts of training and keeping lean muscle tissue are vast, including strength for enjoying all levels of activities, increased hormone profile, sexual enhancement, and looking great!

To keep bones strong,

1. Increase consumption of Vitamin D and Calcium
2. Eliminate smoking, soda, alcohol, excess sodium, and excess caffeine
3. Incorporate Plyometrics and heavy strength training in your workout routines

To preserve your precious muscle tissue,

Strength train with heavy loads, 2-3x/week in a 3-8 rep range (3-4 sets). See Chapter 8 for a template!

Charles Eugster, 95

Charles was a retired dentist who started working out at 85 years old. He went on to win bodybuilding events, rowing events, and Masters track events. His book is called "Age is Just a Number".

CHAPTER 5:
A YOUNG HEART

"Heart Disease could be as rare as malaria
if we just put into practice what we already know."
–Dean Ornish, MD

Heart Disease is the leading cause of death as we age, so it is necessary to address the prime importance of doing what is in your power to keep it healthy! If the health of your heart is not made a priority, statistically, it will kill you. Unless you were born with a heart defect or genetic heart condition, you DO have control over how soon this will happen. Heart disease is caused by **lack of exercise, poor nutrition,** and a **lifestyle that creates physical or psychological stress.** Our society has been well-educated about how these three main lifestyle issues increase heart disease, so I will spare you the monotony of reiterating this information. Let's go on to talk about what you can do to eliminate the three top risk factors!

Exercise for a Healthy Heart

All exercise is beneficial for the health of your heart; however, research shows us that the best program for keeping the heart healthy will involve BOTH strength training and cardiovascular training.

Strength Training increases the pressure in our veins and arteries through the contractions that happen when we exert force and then release it. It increases blood flow to muscles in a way that aerobic activity does not, and needs to be included in any program designed to improve heart health.

Cardiovascular training, popularly referred to as "cardio", can be done at many different intensities and protocols. The most effective form of "cardio" you can do for heart health is interval training. Interval Training is a protocol where you exercise more intensely for 40 sec-1 minute, followed by a recovery interval of 2-4 minutes. Interval training is superior to Steady State Cardio, where you maintain an activity at the same intensity level over time. Many people jog, walk, swim, or bike at lower intensities sustained over 30minutes to an hour without altering intensity levels.

Although steady state cardio is less effective when it comes to burning fat and improving heart health, it still is an important part of a balanced exercise program. Firstly, steady state cardio at a low level is used to help the body recover between more intense workout sessions (such as strength training and intervals). While more intense forms of exercise create oxygen debt and cellular waste as byproducts, low intensity cardio floods the body with oxygen. Your highly oxygenated blood brings nutrients and healing to your cells, has a cleansing effect on brain, body, and spirit!

Secondly, low intensity cardio creates stress reducing and mood boosting hormones to be released into your system. Enjoying a leisurely bike ride, a long walk, a swim, a hike in nature, mowing the yard.... these are all activities that are not strenuous but will elevate your heart rate slightly while you are enjoying yourself.

Nutrition for a Healthy Heart

Over the last few decades, there has been much conflicting information presented to the public about what foods either cause or prevent heart disease. Every couple of years new "research" has been released that sways our beliefs about what we should be eating. Unfortunately, much of the information you are fed does not originate from a desire to improve your health! The research supporting health statements is often funded by major food companies who are looking for a marketing angle.

We were told that eggs raised cholesterol. We were told that saturated fat caused heart disease. We were told not to eat butter. We were told that skim milk was healthier than whole milk. The list could go on as there were many foods that we were led to believe to be "healthy" or "unhealthy". In many cases, we discovered over time that the research was flawed, incomplete, or biased. For example, we now know cholesterol from your diet does not increase blood cholesterol, and we are eating eggs again. Many investigative reports, documentaries, and books are available that expose America's history of food consumption and how certain markets manipulated public understanding of health in order to sell food products. Books like "Big Fat Food Fraud" by Jeff Scot Philips or "Feeding You Lies" by Vani Hari are examples of resources that expose major food companies and the damaging misinformation they have spread to manipulate our purchasing choices.

Many people look to the American Heart Association (AHA) for information and guidance on heart health. At the grocery store, you can find their "heart-healthy" label on food items. The label is a red heart with a white check mark in it. Be aware that the AHA's healthy heart label that is marketed on food products is not trust-worthy. The AHA historically has accepted millions of dollars in donations from food companies. They also make a fortune by "selling" their heart-healthy label. When a manufacturer wants to get a heart-healthy label put on a food product they are selling, they pay thousands of dollars to the AHA *per product* to gain the "heart-check mark" imprimatur (renewable, at a price, every year). In addition, the AHA also accepts millions of dollars in "donations" from major pharmaceutical companies, who push heart medications such as statins.

My intention is not to create a negative vibe around the food industry or AHA, but I do wish to raise your awareness that not all information is coming from pure motives. "Research" that is presented regarding your heart health should be viewed with suspicion if the "findings" will ultimately make money for a food or drug company. If the information sounds highly convincing, do some investigating to discover the source of funding for the research project.

Many people purchase and consume supplements that they believe will improve their heart health. As mentioned in earlier chapters, supplements are not as effective as the product manufacturer leads you to believe! The most effective way to get the vitamins and fats you need to keep a healthy heart is through whole, unadulterated foods! A group of doctors from Johns Hopkins produced an article citing over a dozen studies that showed no improvement in health conditions as a result of supplementation, and that in fact some supplements could be harmful.[13]

---

[13] Guallar, Eliseo, et al. "Enough is Enough: Stop Wasting Money on Vitamin and Mineral Supplements". *Annals of Internal Medicine,* American College of Pysicians, December 17, 2013

Trust the earth. It has no ulterior motives for the beautiful food it produces for you. Food from the earth was not created for financial profit! Food from the earth exists in abundance, and was created to give you life! For the healthiest heart, eat food that comes directly from the earth and has not been altered or tampered with in any way. Follow the *Living Younger* Nutrition Pillar: **Eat Food That Has Life In It**! Ignore marketing claims on food products or supplements. Remember that labels are a marketing strategy and someone is making money from convincing you that their processed, chemically-altered food is going to help your heart! The "heart healthy" box of whole grain pasta sitting on a shelf **cannot** match the life given to your body from a potato produced by the earth.

Your heart will be healthiest when you eat more plant foods (veggies, fruits, roots, natural grains), healthy fats (see list in Chapter 2), and unadulterated, fresh protein sources (fish/fowl/game/meat). A diet widely recommended for heart health is the Mediterranean diet, which includes all the foods on the Living Younger nutrition lists from Chapter 2! Olive oil and other healthy fats, nuts, fresh fish/seafood, vegetables and fruits, and grains are staples in this diet. There are recipe books, informational books, and online resources to help you follow a Mediterranean diet. If you are being proactive about your heart health and want structure and guidance, following a Mediterranean diet may be a good option for you.

Stress

Stress is a main contributing factor to heart disease! Stressful factors alone do not cause heart disease, but rather your response to the stressor. The great news is that your **response** to stress is within your control! You may not be able to control certain factors that may cause stress (for example your boss, your kids, the weather, your neighbors), but you ALWAYS can control your response to stress. I will give you much more information regarding stress in Chapter 7! We will talk about different types of stress, how it effects the body, and how to reduce it.

Summary

All studies, research, and discoveries related to having a healthy heart have found that high quality nutrition, daily exercise, and reduction of stress are the most effective measures to preventing heart disease. The great news is that improvement in these three areas will give you a healthier heart so that you can live longer AND the added benefit is that you will look, feel, and move like you're a decade younger! Daily practice of the secrets to Living Younger will automatically ensure a strong and healthy heart as a byproduct.

With that in mind, here's a quick summary of what we learned in this chapter:

1. Include both Interval Training and Strength training in your exercise program to ensure a healthy heart
2. Eat food that is from the earth (has life in it or was recently alive)
3. Learn how to respond more positively to stressful situations

Dr. Jeffry Life, 72

Dr. Life, miserably out of shape at age 59, changed his life and is now in the best shape of his life at 78. He has written "The Life Plan" as well as other books to help others enjoy youth as well.

CHAPTER 6:
A YOUTHFUL SPIRIT

"Those who love deeply never grow old.
They may die of old age, but they die young."
–Arthur Wing Pinero

A wholistic definition of disease is "Dis-Ease in the body". Disease is simply a body that is not at ease with itself, a body that is not in harmonious flow as it is when we are well. We were given an amazing, intelligent body that is capable of self-healing when given the correct tools and cared for!

I understand that some factors that affect our health we cannot control and I am not presuming that all health or medical issues originate from a spiritual condition. Some health issues we are born with, some are genetic, some come by way of accident, injury, or trauma. My intention is to bring to your awareness that the wellness you feel emotionally and spiritually has a PROFOUND effect on the well-being of your body. Enjoying a body that is at ease starts with creating a spirit that is at peace.

You are Energy

How do we know that the emotional energy you feel effects the cells in your body? Let's examine what Quantum Physicists are revealing about energy and subatomic particles! Quantum Physics is a fascinating, growing field of study that started in the early 1900's and has completely challenged the way we view the world. It has been proven that every piece of matter, when broken down into its smallest possible unit, is vibrating in a field of energy. Quantum physicists discovered that atoms are made up of vortices of energy that are constantly spinning and vibrating, each one radiating its own unique energy signature. When the human body is broken down into atomic particles, we are really just beings of energy and vibration, radiating our own unique energy signature.

Emotions: Energy in Motion

Emotions emit vibrational energies. Each emotion we feel carries a different vibration, which affects us and our surroundings in different ways. In a Japanese study by Dr. Masaru Emoto, water that was exposed to shame, hatred, and disdain reflected damaged and distorted water crystals, while water that was exposed to love and gratitude created beautiful symmetrical crystals! He wrote a New York Times bestseller, titled "The Hidden Messages in Water", which includes pictures of all the water crystals he studied and photographed.

Other studies have shown that plants that were exposed to love and gratitude flourished while those exposed to indifference and disdain withered.

If the cells in water and plants respond to emotional vibrations, how much more the human body responds to the vibrations we experience and allow! The human body is made up of 60% water as well as trillions of bacteria that are alive and sensitive to vibrations. If you want to enjoy a vibrant body, it needs to contain a spirit that can give and receive the highest emotional vibrations on a daily basis, such as love, joy, peace, gratitude, and empathy. When you carry resentment, unforgiveness, guilt, fear, and bitterness in your spirit, your body will show it. These emotions carry low vibrations in the body, and prevent peace or ease.

Below is a scale of low vibrations to high vibrations:

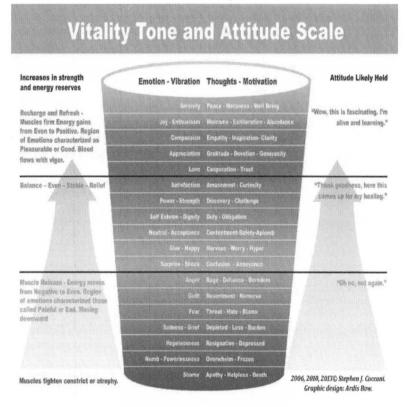

The great news is that you have the ability to choose your vibrational energy by choosing your emotional state! A powerful principle I learned from Steven Covey in his book "Seven Habits of

Highly Effective People" is that in the gap between what happens and how you respond to it is your freedom to choose.

This freedom of choice puts YOU in control of your emotional states. If someone cuts you off on the highway, you can choose your response. You could feel angry, which is a low vibrational energy, or you could feel

> *"If you want to find the secrets to the Universe, think in terms of energy, frequency, and vibration."*
>
> –Nikola Tesla

compassion for the amount of stress or confusion that person is suffering. Look how high compassion is on the energy frequency scale! Evaluate the situations in your life that frequently cause you a low-level response, and let your imagination go for a minute. What would happen if you choose a higher-level emotion the next time this situation occurs? What if your response was acceptance or amusement? There is a cost to living in low-level vibration emotions.

I want to bring special attention to the issue of forgiveness. Many low vibrations such as shame, resentment, blame and hate are tied to unforgiveness. Lack of forgiveness can wreak havoc on our bodies, create chronic dis-ease, and cause people to make harmful choices as they act on these low vibrations.

The Healing Power of Forgiveness

It is crucial for our own health and vitality to forgive those that wronged us. Lack of forgiveness is a poison that kills YOU, not the person who wronged you. It is like holding a hot coal in your hand to throw at someone else, meanwhile it is burning YOUR skin off. Forgive someone, not for THEIR benefit and not because they deserve it, but for YOUR benefit, as the feelings of blame and hate and resentment pull your vibrations down low and make your body sick.

The process of forgiveness involves deciding to remove our attention from the other person, from what they did, haven't done, or need to do. It takes the focus off of them; off waiting for and wanting them to be different. We stop trying to get compassion or acknowledgment from the other, stop trying to get them to see and know our pain and suffering, stop wanting them to be sorry. Forgiveness means that we simply give up the fight to have the other person take responsibility for what they've done, how it affected us, and to make it right. It doesn't even matter if the other party knows that you've forgiven them or not, forgiveness truly is an INSIDE job. We no longer need them to acknowledge us or what they have done. We stop struggling to get something *back* from the other and that allows us to truly be free to take care of ourselves and to offer ourselves the compassion we so crave.

Forgiveness, ultimately, is about freedom. When we need someone else to change in order for us to be okay, we are a prisoner. In the absence of forgiveness, we're shackled to anger and resentment. Remember the mark of being a proactive person is focusing on what we can control: OURSELVES, and not focusing on what we can't control: ANOTHER PERSON.

Even more important than forgiving others is to forgive ourselves. We are loveable human beings capable of great goodness, no matter what actions and choices from the past have caused us to feel guilt/shame/anger/self-hatred. To forgive ourselves, we let go of the "could've should've would've". We release ourselves from our own judgment, shame, self-blame, or wishing things would be different. We give ourselves compassion; see the emotional scale above and notice how high compassion is on the scale of vibrations!

What would you tell your child or best friend if they confided in you something that they beat themselves up about? Use that same compassion, love, and gentle language on yourself. We cannot change the past. Instead, we accept it and stop wishing it were different. When we replay a negative situation/event from the past, it is like watching a bad movie over and over, giving us the chance to feel bad again every time. If we do not forgive and release ourselves or others, we charge our bodies with low vibrations that create disease! What if we turned that movie off, popped it out of the DVD player, THANKED IT for the opportunity to learn from it, then burned it. Only then are we free to focus all our energy on writing a new movie for our future! You will feel 10 lbs. lighter when you do this. There is a great video on forgiveness by Jay Shetty on Vimeo.com, called "Jay Shetty-Forgiveness". Please watch!

I could write a small book on the topic of forgiveness, but there are already many good ones out there for you to use if the lack of forgiveness in your life is resonating with you as an area that needs some focus. My purpose is to guide you to all things that would affect your aging experience, and for that reason I needed to raise your awareness of the devastating effects of unforgiveness so that if it strikes a truth within you, you will know to spend more time and energy healing yourself in this area to experience true vitality.

Gratitude

When people begin to understand how their negative emotions affect them and have the desire to raise their emotional energy, they are often uncertain as to HOW to do so. A great metaphor to help you think of emotional energy involves a glass of water. Imagine a glass half full of water. Let's say the water represents high vibrations such as love, joy, and peace, and the empty half of the jar is low energy such as pain, regret, resentment, unforgiveness. The only way to get rid of the emptiness is to fill up the glass with more water! You can't "fight the emptiness" or make it go away......doing so actually brings more focus to the low vibration emotions and creates more of the negative energy you are trying to move away from.

The way to reduce low vibration emotions is to fill up the glass with high, positive vibrations (more water)! A simple yet highly effective way to add high energy emotions is to start practicing gratitude. Practicing gratitude is easy, fun, and feels so good! Gratitude is one of the highest vibrational energies! Feeling the emotion of gratitude floods your body with positive chemical reactions and actually changes your physiological state. Resentment cannot exist when you are feeling grateful. It disappears, along with the other low, harmful vibrations. Remember, this is a PRACTICE, meaning it may feel awkward or unnatural at first but will grow easier and more automatic over time. Start every day, with 10 minutes of concentrated time, a pen and paper, and allow your heart to feel things you are TRULY grateful for! **Feel it first**, then write it down. **The vibration you feel is more important than the thoughts themselves**. Sometimes when you are feeling and thinking gratitude, you may have an action come to mind, such as "I'll send this person a note and let them know I appreciate them" or "I want to take my wife out tonight to show her how much I appreciate her". Write it down and follow through!

> *"We can only be said to be alive in those moments when our hearts are conscious of our treasures."*
>
> *–Thorton Wilder*

The more you practice gratitude, the easier it will come and in time you will find yourself living in a **state of gratitude**. It will change you profoundly, you will find that there is little room for resentment or jealousy or fear as you feel full each day.

Another practical way you can raise your vibration when you are feeling low vibrational energy is to type in the search box of your internet browser "quotes on gratitude" and allow yourself to slowly think on and soak in some of the quotes (meditate on the quotes). You will find that there are 2 or 3 that really touch you and spark that feeling of gratitude!

Other Ways to Raise Your Vibration

Gratitude practice is the most effective and quickest way to raise your vibrational frequency, however, there are other practical actions you can take that have been proven to raise your vibrational energy:

1. Go barefoot outside! A field of study, called Grounding, shows us that our bare skin in connection with the electrons on the earth surface recharges our bodies and produces numerous beneficial side effects[14].

---

[14]Chevalier, Gaétan, et al. "Earthing: Health Implications of Reconnecting the Human Body to the Earth's Surface Electrons." Journal of Environmental and Public Health, Hindawi Publishing Corporation, 2012, www.ncbi.nlm.nih.gov/pmc/articles/PMC3265077/.

2. Listen to classical music, or music at the frequency of 528hz.

3. Exercise and movement will raise your energies!

4. Dance!

5. Belly Breathe for 5 minutes. (Learn how in the addendum at the end of the book).

6. Laugh! Watch or read something funny, go out with a friend who makes you laugh, or laugh at yourself!

7. "Pray". This word means different things to different people, but the point is that you are committing your concerns to a higher intelligence and then releasing them. It means that you are asking for "x" in faith, and believing it will show up.

8. Listen to a guided meditation. A simple, short meditation to try for starters can be found at Youtube.com, called "5 Minute Guided Meditation for Gratitude".

9. Smile. It actually changes your physiology! Your breathing, your tension levels, your posture, and your blood pressure all change favorably when you smile!

10. Spend time in nature. There are other countries actually terming this "forest bathing", as science is confirming the spiritual and physical benefits of spending time in nature.

When you elevate the vibrational energy you carry, everything in your external reality WILL elevate as well. Your health will improve and your relationships will improve. If you are ready to release pain, to forgive, and/or to heal from past wrongs, consider working with an experienced life coach or counselor. An excellent coach is trained to get you results quicker and more effectively than you can on your own!

Jane Fonda, 75

Jane Fonda, now in her 80s, has been leading a healthy and
fit lifestyle for decades and still looks 20 years younger than
her chronological age.

CHAPTER 7:
A LIFESTYLE OF LEVITY

"We don't stop playing because we grow old,
we grow old because we stop playing."
–George Bernard Shaw

A spirit that can experience levity about life will keep you feeling young forever! Laughter, joy, gratitude, and love are amongst the highest vibrations experienced by humans, as we explored in the previous chapter. Our physiology changes when we experience these emotions! We change the chemicals in our body, and our breathing, posture, digestion, blood pressure, and muscle tension responds! How amazing!

Now, think of your physiology when you are stressed. You use your upper diaphragm (stress breathing) and do not get full oxygen saturation. Your shoulders are carried a few millimeters higher as your neck/shoulder muscles tense up, your eyebrows furrowed. When you are feeling love, your body softens, your heart rate slows, your face relaxes, and you may even sigh deeply (flooding the body with oxygen).

In this era, our lifestyles often prevent us from experiencing levity! We live busy, stressful lives and we strive to measure up to society's standards, our own standards, our boss's standards, and more. We take life seriously. We stop playing.

In this chapter, I want to reveal two major lifestyle behaviors that will rob you of vitality and rapidly age the body. I will then give you the tools to improve these lifestyle issues if you are ready to make a change. The two lifestyle pitfalls we'll be addressing are *stress* and *lack of sleep*.

Stress

Small amounts of stress are helpful to us, and produce hormones and chemical reactions that help us to stay young! One well known hormone that stress produces is Cortisol. Small, *acute* amounts of stress produce benefits such as:

- Keeping us alert and awake by preventing fatigue or brain fog
- Keeping our metabolisms running (it helps us burn fat for energy)
- Balancing blood sugar levels (since it allows cells to take up and use glucose for energy)
- Reducing inflammation and helping with healing
- Balancing fluid levels based on salt and water intake
- Contributing to control over blood pressure
- Helping with many cognitive processes like learning and memory formulation
- Allowing us to respond to and escape perceived dangers

Acute Stress

Acute stress refers to situations and events that can be resolved and eliminated. Acute stress could be self-imposed such as a personal goal, or a deadline at work, or a circumstance such as an unexpected financial expense or family/relationship conflict. These situations can be resolved and are then eliminated. The cortisol is eliminated from our systems in healthy ways such as exercise, breathwork, satisfaction from resolving the challenge, or meditation.

In primitive days, cortisol allowed us to survive and was mostly acute, arising from short-term situations such as chasing prey or being chased by predators, building emergency shelters in severe weather, or escaping natural disasters. Cortisol was naturally eliminated through our bodies during the high-intensity activities we did to mitigate the stressful situations. Our current lifestyles often do not include activities that allow cortisol to flush from our systems, and this hormone can build up over time. We also create lifestyles that cause us to experience chronic stress.

Chronic Stress

Chronic stress is a silent killer. It creates tension in cells and muscle fascia, restricts breathing, and creates narrow thinking. Prolonged exposure to stress creates metabolic damage as it steals vital building blocks for other helpful hormones (testosterone, progesterone, HGH) and converts them into use for cortisol. Our bodies treat cortisol as a survival hormone, and the others as luxury hormones, so in the presence of stress you will not be able to produce adequate "fountain of youth" hormones! Stress and Heart Disease have a strong correlation to each other, and there are many other health problems that are caused by chronically high cortisol levels including diabetes, depression, and a host of digestive issues. Below is a list of symptoms you may experience if you have chronically elevated levels of Cortisol in your body:

- weight gain, especially around the abdomen/stomach (this can happen despite not changing your diet or exercise routine)
- a puffy, flushed face
- mood swings and increased anxiety
- fatigue (including feeling "tired but wired")
- trouble sleeping normally
- irregular periods and fertility problems (chronic stress steals building blocks needed to produce other helpful hormones)
- high blood pressure levels
- acne or other changes in the skin
- higher rates of bone fractures and osteoporosis
- muscle aches and pains
- decreased libido
- higher susceptibility to infections

Chronic stress is a result of a lifestyle that contains prolonged stressful situations that do not get resolved. For example, an individual may have a demanding career, be spending more money than they are making, and have a conflictual relationship with their spouse. Let's say they also have a few kids at home and are sleeping less than 6 hours each night. This is a recipe for dis-ease! Many people will spend a decade or two in a prolonged, stressful life situation like this.

Chronic stress in the body can be experienced even if an individual does not have stressful circumstances! If a person **perceives** an event to be stressful and experiences high levels of anxiety, the body will release Cortisol. The body cannot tell the difference between reality and imagination, so it will kick off the same stress hormones whether an event actually happens or whether you are just feeling anxious about it happening.

For example, if you are hiking and you perceive a snake on the path, your body will release a flood of chemicals to prepare you to fight or flight! Your heartrate will jump, you may feel instantly sweaty, your breathing will increase and become shallow, your pupils will dilate, and you may have the urge to jump up into a tree! When you get closer, you may discover that the long, wriggly object was only a vine, branch, rope......but the perception of a snake already created a physiological response.

Another example could be if you are dreading a conversation with someone, say a co-worker or your boss at work. If you perceive this conversation you are facing as highly stressful, you will get a dose of Cortisol released even if the conversation does NOT turn out to be stressful. Again, our brain responds to our perception of a situation, whether real or imagined.

To fully experience health and vitality you can both reduce the chronically stressful situations in your life AND/OR manage your PERCEPTION of those situations.

Courageously Facing-off With Stress

To live a life full of vitality, we cannot live in chronic stress. One of my favorite quotes by Eckhart Tolle referring to difficult life situations is "Leave the situation, change the situation, or accept it. All else is madness".[15] Many times we settle for "madness", meaning we complain, grit our teeth and tolerate, or worry and have anxiety over the situation. This is not healthy! If you are currently experiencing stress or anxiety about a situation, it is time to take action.

A Writing Exercise

First, write down the situations/relationships that cause you stress and anxiety. There is a courageous action you can take in each of these situations that will provide you with health and freedom long-term! In this section, I will present three pathways to reducing the stress associated with the life situation you wrote down, and encourage you to decide the best path for you, then TAKE ACTION! The three ways you can escape your "madness" are:

a. Leave the situation
b. Change the situation
c. Accept the situation and find gratitude for it

All three of these actions require courage! Leaving a situation is never easy, but the courage comes from making a decision that you will be better if the toxic person/situation is no longer stealing the positive energy you have to give to others and to the world! Face the fears you are stuffing down about leaving a situation, deal with

---

[15] Tolle, E. (1991) The Power of Now. Vancouver B.C., Canada: Namaste Publishing Inc.

them head-on. Write down the fears you have about leaving a situation. Yes, people will be disappointed if you leave the committee, yes, someone will be hurt/disappointed if you end a relationship, yes, your colleagues may be upset if you leave the job. However, if the fear of leaving a stressful situation is the only thing keeping you there, you are literally paying for it with your life. An excellent book for making tough decisions about Leaving/ending a situation is "Necessary Endings" by Dr. Henry Cloud.

Changing a situation takes courage, as there is always resistance to change both from yourself and from others who may be benefitting from the current situation. If leaving a stressful situation is not an option, in what ways can you change it to alleviate stress? Get into a place of high vibrations (positive emotions) and then write down as many options as you can think of, even if some of them are ridiculous. Our brain is AMAZING and will produce solutions when we are not in a restricted state of thinking. Stress and low vibrations like anxiety give us tunnel vision where we cannot see all options. In a state of gratitude, write down what YOU can do about the situation to change it. Do you need to change yourself? This could mean having better boundaries, or improving your skill level, or working with a coach to improve a relationship. It could mean getting resources (books, podcasts, seminars) to acquire knowledge. It could mean changing your perspective of a person or situation. Do you need to become better in a certain area? Do you need to make a change organizationally? Do you need to delegate more? Do you need to buy a solution? Take courage, and **take action**. An excellent book to help you take charge of your life and change yourself and your situation is "7 Habits of Highly Effective People" by Stephen Covey.

Accepting a situation with gratitude takes courage as well. Acceptance simply means that you STOP RESISTING! If you determine that leaving or changing a situation will not be an option for you, then stop fighting the situation internally, **stop wishing it were different than what it is,** and look for the gift that you might be missing. You can even thank the situation for giving you the ability to be strong, to learn and to grow. An excellent book to help you with acceptance is "The Power of Now" By Eckert Tolle.

Remember this concept from chapter one: the more focus you give to what you CAN control, the healthier and happier you will be. We called this proactive living. If you have a situation in your life causing you stress, stop waiting for the other person to change. Stop hoping the situation will change. Stop putting your health and well-being in someone else's hands. Thoughts such as "If only my boss would ___" or "if only my spouse would ___" or "if only the kids weren't so ___" reveal a focus on factors you cannot control! I want to empower you to focus on the only factor you can control, which is yourself! You decide: Leave, Change, or Accept. These choices are all within your power, the power to create an amazing future for yourself independent of external factors. These choices will free you from the chronically stressful situations that are damaging your body, your health, and your vitality.

A Case Study

A client of mine was struggling with obesity and experiencing multiple health issues while living a chronically stressful lifestyle. One of the stressors was an elderly parent living in the home, who needed a lot of care and supervision.

This individual carried guilt and worry every time the parent was left alone too long, and was trying to manage the care of the parent in the midst of career, other family members, self-care, and marriage while feeling defeated about their personal goals and watching their health slip away. This stressful situation had been tolerated for several years and the only thing changing was my client's deteriorating health and body. I was watching a slow death.

In this situation, let's review three options this client could choose to reduce one of the chronic stressors:

1. **Leave the situation**. Severing ties is not an option in this case as the elderly parent is loved and cherished.
2. **Change the situation**. Many options here! Hire an in-home caretaker, delegate care to other family members, admit parent to adult care facility while regularly bringing home for visits, get a less demanding career to have more time to care for the parent, and there would be several more creative solutions we could come up with!
3. **Accept the situation**. This means accepting the responsibility of full-time care, with a heart of gratitude. It means refusing to feel victimized as you honor the choice you made. It means the cessation of all complaining about the situation, and instead feeling good daily about the strength and ability you have to care for your loved one and the sacrifices you are choosing to make.

Making any choice above alleviates stress and low vibration emotions, and allows this individual to have more health in their spirit and body. Making NO decision IS choosing... choosing to be stressed and exhausted and full of complaints. This is the "madness" described by Eckhart Tolle.

My challenge to you is to look closely at your lifestyle and become aware of situations you complain about regularly or that create more low-vibration emotions than high-vibration emotions (refer to the scale). You need a pen and paper, and you need to write down a way out of your "madness". Think through the options of 1. leave, 2. change, or 3. accept. Choose one, write it down, and write down a plan of how you will execute it. It will not be easy to change, leave, or accept some of our difficult life situations. If it was, you would have done it already! You have to have enough pain associated with the reality of what you will lose or sacrifice in your life, body, and level of vitality if you continue in stress, AND an amazing and compelling view of what life will be like for the next few decades if you make some changes now!

I highly recommend working with a life coach or counselor through this process. Again, any of the above choices for reducing stress takes a tremendous amount of courage and support. You will enjoy the process and have support working with someone who is trained to help you!

Sleep

A lack of sleep is also a major lifestyle problem that will rob both the quality and quantity of your years. Here's what happens when you sleep less than 7-9 hours/night.

- It has a negative effect on good bacteria in the gut, which causes malabsorption and inflammation
- It depresses the body's ability to manufacture youth hormones

- It decreases sex drive
- It promotes muscle loss
- It impairs mood and thinking abilities
- It decreases the body's ability to heal itself
- It causes weight gain
- It suppresses the immune system
- It increases risk of diabetes and heart disease.

We know about these harmful side effects! Our health professionals and wellness educators have given us this information, so why is it that we would settle for less sleep and all of the terrible side effects that accompany it? Why would we sacrifice our health, youth, and vitality?

There are two main reasons why people don't get enough sleep— bad bedtime habits and insomnia— and I'll break these down in the next two sections.

Creating Better Bedtime Habits

If you are getting less than 8 hours because of your bedtime habits, the following tips are for you! Many of us have gotten into bad habits of winding down a stressful, tightly scheduled day with screen time, whether watching an hour of TV, browsing the internet, or checking social media and email. It is easy to lose track of time while being entertained in this way, which gets us into bed later than we want. Also, the screens from these electronic devices emit blue light, which suppresses melatonin twice as long as other types of light! This means that when we do get into bed, it will be harder to fall asleep right away. Nightly screen-time use can be a tough lifestyle habit to break. You will need to be intentional in making new bedtime habit changes if you are committed to getting more sleep!

First, decide that you are committed to getting more sleep (specify the amount). Read the list of what happens to your body and health if you keep sacrificing that extra hour of sleep. There are very few things in life worth these negative consequences. Losing an hour of screen time is an easy sacrifice to eliminate all of these side-effects! Breaking an addictive lifestyle pattern is hard, so if you want to do it, you will need to be drastic at first.

Steps to make an earlier bedtime habit

1. Decide you want that extra hour of sleep at all cost. You are no longer willing to sacrifice your health, youth, vitality, sexual performance, and mental acumen for screen time.

2. Be intentional. Set an alarm on your device for 8.5-9 hours before your wake-up time. When this goes off, the device goes into a designated storage area you decide. If you use your cell phone as an alarm clock, make sure you place it next to an outlet far from your bed. Then, begin your normal bedtime routine so that you wind up in the bed about 8 hours before wake-time.

3. Stay consistent. It may take a month before this starts to feel normal and you make a new lifestyle habit. During that month, you will notice your mood and energy levels increase, that you are thinking clearer, and will probably enjoy more connection and intimacy with your partner at the end of the day.

Overcoming Insomnia

The second reason that people do not get enough sleep is because they cannot sleep. They may go to bed in time for a good 7-8 hour stretch, but may experience insomnia that keeps them up for several hours. It could be falling asleep, staying asleep, or waking up very early and not being able to go back to sleep. If you fall in this second group of people, you already know that you need sleep! You probably have taken steps to try to get more sleep and are frustrated that it is elusive.

Causes of Insomnia could be physical or psychological. Here are some steps to take if you are failing to get 7-9 hours of quality sleep because of insomnia. They are categorized into two causes. You may be experiencing both or just one.

Physical Causes of Insomnia

Sometimes a physical factor such as our metabolism, a hormone imbalance, a medication, or your sleeping environment make it hard to sleep. Here are a few things to check for!

1. **Check any medications you are taking**. Many prescription drugs can interfere with sleep, including antidepressants, stimulants for ADHD, corticosteroids, thyroid hormones, high blood pressure medications, and some contraceptives. Common over-the-counter culprits include cold and flu medications that contain alcohol, pain relievers that contain caffeine (Midol, Excedrin), diuretics, and diet pills. If you are taking any of these, look for more natural alternatives! Talk to your doctor or a naturopath about changes

you could make in diet/exercise to eliminate the need for these medications and their harmful side effects.

2. **Change what you eat and drink before bed**. Drinking alcohol may help you fall asleep, but will interfere with your sleep cycle once asleep. *Living Younger* nutritional benefits come from only 8 oz. red wine anyway, so drink this earlier in the evening if it's something you enjoy. Fountain of Youth principal regarding coffee is less than 16 oz. per day. If you are taking in more than this, it will affect your sleep. If you are staying within the 16oz, make sure you've stopped 6-7 hours before bedtime. Even decaffeinated coffee still contains caffeine!

   Eating large meals before bedtime will cause your body to exert its energy on digestion and metabolism while you are sleeping instead of focusing its energy on repair and regeneration. For high quality sleep, meals should be 2-3 hours before bedtime (the larger the meal, the more time needed for digestion while awake). Also, eating or drinking sugars or carbs before bed will cause a spike in blood sugar, then a release of insulin, and usually result in you needing to wake up to use the bathroom 3-4 hours into your sleep. If you are hungry at night, eat a small snack high in fat (less than 200 calories). Examples are 2 TBSP of nut butter, a handful of nuts, ½ a small avocado, 2 eggs, or a ½ cup of full-fat Greek yogurt. Allow 1 hour to digest this before you go to sleep.

3. **Change your environment**. Keep the bedroom **cool and dark** (like a cave!). Make it your sleep sanctuary! Don't do activities in your bedroom such as exercise, work, paying bills, or having heated discussions (on the phone, on skype, or in person). If you have an office area or computer in

your bedroom, move it out! Your brain should associate your bedroom with rest, sleep, and sex.

If you do use screens at night, make sure you are not using screens an hour before bed as the blue light that enters your eyes affects your brain and suppresses its ability to produce Melatonin.

4. **Exercise.** The Sleep Foundation has examined several studies in which individuals with chronic insomnia were able to fall asleep faster, sleep longer, and sleep more deeply with exercise, specifically moderate aerobic exercise.

If you are having trouble sleeping, first check these above "easy fixes". If there are some physical factors you can change, take action! Give your body the environment it needs to do what it wants: Rest and recover through deep sleep!

Mental and Emotional Causes of Insomnia

Anxiety, stress, and depression are some of the most common causes of chronic insomnia. Other common emotional and psychological causes include worry, grief, anger, bipolar disorder, and trauma. Treating these underlying problems is essential to resolving your insomnia.

If you are practicing the *Living Younger* principals, you already will be drastically improving the way you feel physically and emotionally! All the previous chapters regarding raising your vibrations (including forgiveness and gratitude), reducing stressful lifestyle habits, and upgrading your nutrition habits will already be taking hold in your life if you have begun to practice them, so you should also notice an improvement in your sleep. If you want to try a few additional sleep remedies on your own related to anxiety and in-somnia, here is what is proven to help.

Actions you can do to allow sleep

1. **Write down, with pen and paper, the thoughts that are cycling through your head.** If you are lying in bed with thoughts running through your mind, write down the worries, fears, and any other thoughts you have that are creating anxiety or stress. This helps them transition out of your mind, your eyes see them on paper and your brain allows you to release them. Keep a note-book beside your bed!

2. **Practice gratitude through writing.** (We talked about this in Chapter 6). Interrupt your low-level vibrations of anxiety by taking 10 minutes to feel and write down what you are grateful for. This brings ease to your body.

3. **Focus on relaxation instead of sleep.** Here are three tips I recommend:

•   Practice deep belly breathing for 5 minutes

•   Perform muscle tensing followed by relaxation as follows: Lie flat on your back in bed. Starting with your feet, tense the muscles as tightly as you can. Hold for a count of 10, and then relax. Continue to do this for every muscle group in your body, working your way up from your feet to the top of your head.

•   Listen to a guided meditation on either sleep or relaxation (you can look these up on YouTube). Lay on your back with your eyes closed and earphones in. Follow the imagery, breathing, and relaxation the meditation guides you through!

If you are wanting to get more sleep and have been unable to, I en-courage you to run through the checklists of both physical and psychological factors. Sleep is such a beautiful gift, and I wish for you to have as much of it as you want!

Play!

In addition to lowering chronic stress and getting great sleep, another way to keep levity in your life is to play! This will take years off of you and raise your vibrations instantly! **Play is a purposeless activity that brings about joy and pleasure.** That means you're *not* engaged for the sole purpose of winning, accomplishing a goal, or improving yourself. You're simply immersed in the moment-to-moment experience AND enjoying it.

There are many ways to play if you have already stopped or can't remember how. At first you will need to be intentional about playing, and this will feel awkward. Some of the items on the list will make you feel SILLY and WEIRD, but THAT IS THE POINT! Would you rather be silly, or old? Don't take yourself too seriously! Creating levity in your life means that you can laugh at yourself. We learn best about play by watching children.

Here are several ways to play if you've forgotten how!

1. Spend time with kids, engage in their imaginative play.
2. Skip, hopscotch, jump-rope, hula hoop, throw frisbee, swing at a park, blow bubbles. Yeah, you'll feel weird at first, but you won't feel old!
3. The next time you make a mistake, laugh at yourself, shake your head and say "Duh!"
4. Create! Just for fun, no thoughts of perfection or success! (paint, draw, color, make something in your tool shop, make some music, cook something new, make a sand castle, create a fairy garden)

5. Watch silly YouTube videos (look up "try not to laugh") or the cartoon channel.
6. Sing Karaoke
7. Play games, not to win, but for fun! Kickball, bingo, twister, foosball, air hockey, ping pong, hide and seek, card games, etc. As long as you are not trying to "crush it", and are just enjoying the game for what it is, it still counts as play!
8. Have a bubble-gum blowing competition
9. Join a drum circle, community theater or Improv group
10. Dance, you don't even have to look good. In fact, laugh at yourself 😊

Summary

Stress, lack of sleep, and the absence of play in your life will age your body and your spirit. If you have been living a chronically stressful lifestyle, I hope this chapter inspires you to reduce stress, to restore your sleep, and to play more often! I hope that you feel empowered to make changes, starting tonight, to create a lifestyle that brings you joy and levity!

Here's a quick summary of what we learned in this chapter about how to create a lifestyle that allows vitality:

1. Eliminate chronic stress from your life. Make a tough decision to either Leave, Change, or Accept the situations/people causing them.
2. Evaluate the reason/s you may not be getting 7-9 hours per night of sleep. Implement some of the strategies I've shared with you to protect this most precious vitality tool!
3. Play!

Johanna Quaas, 86
Johanna Quaas, a 90-year-old gymnast (Visit
https://youtu.be/7NZ6C6wGpAE to see one of her routines!).

CHAPTER 8: EXERCISE, THE KEY TO YOUTH

"Getting old is not a matter of age. It's a lack of movement.
And the ultimate lack of movement is death."
–Anthony Robbins

Exercise, or intentional physical movement, is the **key** to preserving youth in your body! All of the systems in the human body thrive with movement. Your mobility, bone health, muscle tissue, ability to reduce cortisol, higher emotional vibrations, healthy heart, great looking body and libido all benefit from physical exercise! In fact, the less we move, the closer to death we are. Of all the secrets in this book, your commitment to daily exercise would have the greatest impact on your ability to stay young!

We talked about setting standards for yourself in Chapter One. The standard of *daily* movement has to be raised to an **ABSOLUTE MUST** as you age. Do not think of exercise as an option or a bonus or a "should" or a luxury for people who have time. It is a "must" for you. Yes, it will cost you 20-60 minutes per day, but the alternative is that it will cost you your freedom in your later years. Without spending those daily 20-60 minutes of movement now, you will be spending

> *"Man sacrifices his health in order to make money. Then he sacrifices his money to recuperate his health".*
> –Dalai Lama

your resources (time and money) in your later years attempting to regain the health and vitality you lost.

Your body gives you freedom to experience life. It is your vehicle to carry out the wishes, goals, and desires that you have. Some of our richest life experiences are fulfilled by our ability to move! Freedom in movement is needed to be the kind of lover you want to be, to be the kind of grandparent you want to be, to experience new adventures, to be a helpful volunteer, or to travel and explore the world.

The Importance of Movement

Movement is a privilege. If you are healthy enough today to move, you are blessed with a beautiful gift. Do not take this for granted! There are thousands of people sitting in wheelchairs or lying in hospital beds today that would give anything to have the privilege of movement. The old adage "Use it or Lose it" is 100% true when it comes to movement. If we do not exercise, with intentionality, we slowly lose the ability to do so! Sometimes we have a sense of entitlement about our body. We feel it should just work for us every day, pain free, the way we want it to, without investing time and energy in it, nor taking care of it, or nor working on it. To quote Andrew Carnegie, "Anything in life worth having is worth working for". MOVEMENT IS A PRIVILEGE. We lose that privilege if we are poor stewards of it.

In this chapter I will show you how to exercise your body so that you can enjoy the freedom and privilege of movement for decades to come!

Health vs. Fitness

It is important to clarify that there is a difference between being Healthy, and being Fit. Health and Fitness are not the same thing. **Health** is a state of complete well-being, where the body, mind, and soul are free of disease and at peace. Health provides high quality of life, freedom from pain, low stress levels, and longevity. **Fitness** relates to one's ability to perform physical activity. Fitness requires you to raise the limits of strength, endurance, speed, flexibility, power, and coordination in the body for the purpose of enhanced performance, competition, or physique.

With that in mind, let's take a look at a graphic that illustrates the differences and similarities between the two:

FITNESS versus HEALTH

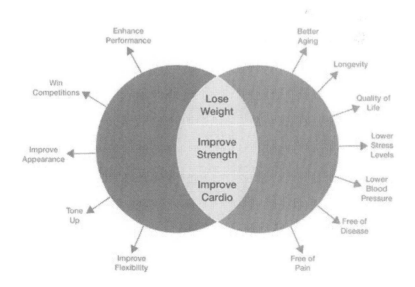

The best workout program to maintain optimal health must be very well-balanced. If your goals are **fitness** related such as muscle gain, losing body fat, endurance training, training for a sport or training to be able to lift certain amounts of weight, then you would need a different program than the one described in this book. The above mentioned are examples of **fitness** goals, and although there is some crossover (as noted in the graphic), your fitness goals will not necessarily make you healthier or have a younger life experience. Each of the fitness goals I just described will require a separate goal-specific program, as they are training more isolated facets of the body's systems.

Workouts designed for fitness goals fail to bring total health as these workouts strain one system while neglecting another. For example, a person training to increase muscle size will tax very different systems than a person training to run a 5k race. The person training to gain muscle size may sacrifice their joint mobility and cardiovascular fitness. The person training for a 5k will sacrifice some muscle mass, joint health, and hormone profile. These fitness goals do not create overall health, and many times lead to pain and dysfunction in the body if not balanced.

That said, I AM A BIG FAN OF FITNESS GOALS! They are exciting, provide a feeling of growth and accomplishment, and create a sense of pride. Personally, I love having fitness goals! As a Masters athlete who competes in track and field, I train for the majority of the year with the goal of becoming faster and stronger so that I perform better in my events! I have learned to switch my focus back to health goals during my off season, to have a break from fitness goals, so that I can allow for healing and wholeness.

Exercises that Promote Vitality

For the purpose of this book, I will share with you the types of exercises that will give you optimal HEALTH, not optimum fitness. We will use fitness as a vehicle to obtain a disease free, pain free body that moves well. These exercises must be organized into a well-rounded program and must include:

- Exercises to stimulate an increase in bone density (plyos and strength training)
- Exercises to stimulate the **muscles** for strength, hormone profile, and physique (strength training)
- Full functional movement to increase **joint mobility** (mobility exercises)
- Cardiovascular exercises to strengthen the **heart** (Level 1, Level 2 cardio and strength training)

Let's get started with a deeper look into all of these exercise modalities, starting with Cardiovascular Training (cardio).

Level-1 Activity

In the exercise program in Chapter 9, you will notice a reference to Level-1 cardio activity. Level-1 activity refers to any steady paced, low intensity activity done for 45 minutes to 1 hour (start with 30 min if you are not currently active). On a scale of 1-10, with 1 being no exertion and 10 being maximal, this activity should be done around 4-5, and should be enjoyable! You should be able to carry on a conversation during this level of activity. This form of exercise was mentioned in Chapter 5 as a form of exercise that promotes a healthy heart (as well as reduces stress!). We include this type of exercise 2x per week for these reasons:

- low intensity efforts circulate highly oxygenated blood all through the body and help with muscle recovery from more intense workouts, and the healing/detoxifying of cells!
- low intensity efforts give the body a pathway to burn off cortisol and stress-related toxins, while releasing beneficial hormones to elevate mood and energy such as endorphins
- many low intensity efforts can be done outdoors. Research has shown that being in nature has many positive effects on your brain, spirit, and physiology as well as reducing Cortisol.

Examples of Level-1 Activity
- Hiking
- Biking
- Rowing
- Gardening/using a push mower
- Swimming
- Elliptical machine
- Walking
- Cross country skiing
- Dancing
- Yoga
- Pilates
- Easy Jog (if you are already running)

Level-2 Activity

Level-2 activity refers to activities done in short, high intensity intervals or bursts. This means maximal exertion (on a scale of 1-10, an 8.5-9.5) done for anywhere between 20-45 seconds followed by a rest period of 2-4 minutes, done for 6-8 rounds. The entire workout (including a warmup) will take you less than 30 minutes! High Intensity Intervals will provide the following benefits:

- Dramatically increases the production of Human Growth Hormone!
- Causes the release of other hormones such as adrenaline and testosterone, as well as endorphins
- Is very effective at burning fat while preserving muscle
- Strengthens the cardiovascular system
- Takes ½ the amount of time of other workouts to produce high quality benefits

---

Examples of Level-2 Activity

- Sprint up a hill for 30 seconds, walk back down and rest for a total of 3 minutes. Repeat 6-8x
- Swim one pool length at maximum speed, walk or slow stroke back to the start. Repeat 10x
- Bike or row as hard as you can, on medium-high resistance, for 40 seconds. Recover for 2 minutes. Repeat 8x
- Put elliptical machine on high resistance and go hard for 30 seconds, set back to low resistance to recover for 2 minutes. Repeat 6-8x
- Jump rope for 30 seconds, walk or step on/off step for 2 minutes to recover. Repeat 8x

---

Tabata Intervals

A special note on an interval exercise protocol by a Japanese doctor, Izumi Tabata, called Tabata Intervals. The term "Tabata" is used loosely these days in bootcamps and group exercises classes, so I wish to educate you on what this interval protocol actually involves. The initial Tabata interval workout from the study in 1996 was performed on stationary bicycles. The researchers examined two groups of amateur athletic males in their mid-twenties.[16] The first group pedaled on an ergometer for sixty minutes at moderate intensity, similar to a long jogging session.

The second group pedaled at maximal effort for 20 seconds, followed by 10 seconds of rest, for 4 minutes (completing 7 to 8 sets total). The key phrase is *maximal effort*, as each interval was expected to be a sprint. If athletes could not keep up the speed requirements, they were stopped at 7 sets.

Both groups worked out for a grand total of 5 days a week. However, the first group worked out for 5 hours a week and the second group only worked out for 20 minutes a week! For both groups, the protocol lasted for 6 weeks. The second group (the sprint-interval group) showed more improvement than the first group (the steady-state group) in ANAEROBIC capacity, but even more surprising also showed the same improvement in AEROBIC capacity as well! Thus, it seems that a four-minute maximal intensity Tabata workout had the same aerobic benefits as doing a sixty-minute

---

[16]Tabata, I. , "Effects of moderate-intensity endurance and high-intensity intermittent training on anaerobic capacity and ˙VO2max", *Medicine & Science in Sports and Exercise,* October 1996.

moderate intensity workout. The research was pretty shocking in that you could get two-in-one benefits from only a **four-minute workout**.

The key to using this tool effectively is to keep intensity very high, a 10, and to use a safer, low impact activity such as stationary bike (the original research was done on bikes), row machine, or swim.

Strength Training

Any activity that applies resistance to a muscle during contraction can produce an increase in strength! In previous chapters we have talked about all of the amazing benefits that come from strength training! It shows up at the top of the list for preventing heart disease, reducing stress, creating a healthier metabolism, upgrading your hormone profile, increasing your strength and libido, improving your posture, and creating lean, sexy muscle!

There are many different ways to strength train! Firstly, there are a wide variety of tools you can use to apply resistance to your muscles. You could use your own bodyweight against gravity or an external load such as dumbbells, kettlebells, barbells, weighted vests, machines, or resistance bands.

Secondly, you can use different types of muscle contractions to build strength. You can hold a contraction without movement (think of performing a plank or holding a squat position), you can shorten a muscle through movement (think of pulling your chin up to the bar in a pullup) or you can lengthen a muscle through movement (lowering yourself from the bar in a pullup).

A third factor to consider in how you will strength train is the amount of repetitions, the number of sets, and the amount of rest time you take in between muscle contractions. This third factor has the biggest impact on how the muscle will adapt! For the purposes of building vitality and strength for a high-quality of life, most of the strength training you will perform will happen in a 4-8 repetition range with 1-2 minutes rest in between sets (total of 3-4 sets). In Chapter 9, I will give you a strength training template with prescribed set, reps, and rest periods.

I practice, coach, and highly recommend *functional strength training*. Functional strength training differs from traditional strength training in several ways. Functional training uses **full-body** exercises so that you get higher amounts of muscle activation and intramuscular coordination. When you strength train in functional movement patterns you not only gain strength, you receive the additional benefits of coordination and balance! Training with full body exercises is the best way to build a younger, more functional body AND takes much less time than a traditional routine!

Understanding Functional Training

Many traditional strength training exercises involve activating one muscle group at a time, keeping the rest of the body's muscles deactivated while that one muscle is working. Exercises may involve sitting on a machine or a bench while isolating the muscle of focus. This is an old model from the bodybuilding community, as competitors singled out small accessory muscles to create muscle shape, tone, mass, and definition in their physiques. They were training their body for a "Fitness Goal", for size and definition. The traditional strength training model does not serve the goal of producing a strong, functional body with high levels of mobility and coordination.

The human body was designed to work together! Our core is designed to be activated when we are standing upright and lifting something heavy with our legs while grasping the object with our arms. Human movement is designed to be an amazing coordination of the body's muscles! Climbing, jumping, sprinting, reaching, carrying heavy items, chopping wood, all of these complex movements involve strength in all parts of the body, the ability to activate as much muscle as possible, and the ability to coordinate these muscles to work together! As we strength train to have an amazing aging experience, it is important to do exercises that integrate the whole body and activate as much muscle as possible. This is functional training.

Let's compare traditional vs. functional strength training for the chest muscles. In a traditional strength training exercise for the chest, a person might sit on a machine at the gym to do a chest press. The whole core and lower body are deactivated as the person sits in the seat while only the chest/triceps/shoulders are working. The adjustable levers of the machine are set to attempt to fit the lengths of the arms and torso, and then your movement pattern is locked into the hinge pattern of the machine.

Now consider functional training for the chest, where a person might lie down on a bench with a dumbbell in each hand to do a bench press. Your feet are planted, glutes engaged, core braced, and your neuromuscular system is working hard to stabilize 2 free dumbbells in a coordinated pressing movement! There are so many more muscles activated and integrated!

Let's look at the bicep muscle and compare how we would strengthen it in using a traditional exercise compared to using a functional exercise. In a traditional strength exercise, you might spend 5 minutes doing 3-4 sets of bicep curls with a dumbbell to strengthen the bicep, a small muscle in your upper arm. In functional training, you could perform sets of pull-ups (whether pulling your full bodyweight, modified, or assisted). When you perform any version of a pullup, not only are the biceps activated and strengthened, but ALSO you synergistically activate the core, lats, and upper back (and increase grip strength)! Now THAT is an efficient use of your time!

These are just a few examples of the difference between functional and traditional strength training. Below, I provide a list of my favorite functional exercises for strength training that will give you the biggest return on your time and the greatest benefit to your body.

One other note about a balanced Living Younger strength training workout is that you need to be intentional to balance the front and back of the body. The "mirror muscles" in the front of the body, such as chest, biceps, quads and abs, tend to get more focus because we can see them. However, training in an unbalanced way over time will create muscle and strength imbalances that will predispose you to injuries. For every exercise you do for the front of your body, there should be at least 1 exercise for the back of your body. These can be better classified as movement patterns. A "Push" primarily involves the front of the body while a "Pull" primarily involves the back of the body. We want to create balanced strength in our ability to both push and pull!

Multi-Joint Functional Strength Training Exercises*	
Upper Body Pull • Pullups** • Bodyweight rows, all varieties (TRX, equalizer bars, squat rack bar) • 1 arm dumbbell rows • Bent over barbell rows • Bent over reverse flys	**Upper Body Push** • Bench press, all varieties (barbell, dumbbell, kettlebell, single arm, both arms, incline) • Military press standing/kneeling • Tricep dips • Pushups of all varieties
Lower Body Pull (Backside) • Deadlifts of all variations! (kettlebell, barbell, dumbbell, hex bar, single leg, double leg, etc.) • Hamstring curls (use a ball, a TRX, or sliders) • Hip bridges of all variations • Squats done correctly (glutes)	**Lower Body Push (Front Side)** • Lunges of all variations (all directions, loaded with barbell, dumbbell, kettlebell, vest) • Weighted step-ups • Single leg sit-downs • Split squats

*All of the above exercises describe a pattern of movement and have multiple variations!

**As many people cannot do pullups with their bodyweight, there are many variations and ways to assist a pullup! What counts is the movement of a pullup done a load of 4-8 reps to failure, no matter how much assistance you need.

<u>Other important full body strength exercises to include:</u>
Turkish Get-Up varieties
Heavy Carrying of all varieties

Plyometrics (Plyos)

Plyometrics are a category of exercises in which a muscle is rapidly stretched then contracted (activated), creating an explosive movement. Plyometrics are graded on a scale of low-level impact to high level impact, and should always be started at a low level to allow bones, joints, muscles and CNS (central nervous system) to adapt. An example of a low-level plyometric exercise is jumping rope, while a high level plyo could be jumping up onto a box.

Plyometric exercises engage the whole body and when practiced consistently over time, will give you the feeling of being agile and quick! The benefits of this type of exercise are development of power and quick reaction (neuromuscular adaptation). Another benefit of plyos is an increase in bone density. This is an adaptation the body makes to the small amount of stress placed on the musculoskeletal system when exposed to impact. Including plyometric exercises in your routine is important in the prevention of falls, as you are building stronger bones, better balance and reaction time, neuromuscular coordination, and agility.

Examples of Plyometric Exercises	
Low Impact Level	*High Impact Level*
• Jump Rope	• Box Jumps
• Skipping	• Broad Jumps
• Agility Ladder Drills	• Single Leg Bounding
• Hopping	• Depth Jumps
• High-Knee Jog in place	• Hurdle Hops
• Medicine Ball throws (wall ball or chest pass	• Tuck Jumps
• Squat Jumps	• Clap Pushups
• Push Press	

Mobility Routine

A mobility routine is a series of movements that will take your joints through their full range of motion in a gentle, easy flow. In Chapter 3 we learned of the great importance of maintaining your mobility through the rest of your life, and how it needed to be practiced daily! There are several positions that will give you the greatest return for your time investment, which I have listed below.

Two highly effective positions, one for overall upper body mobility and the other for overall lower body mobility, are **hanging** and **deep squatting**. There is a whole body of research on hanging, the amazing effects it has on the shoulder as well as decompressing the spinal discs. It will open space in the shoulder and actually improve your posture and shoulder structure if done consistently over time, PLUS increase your grip strength. Deep squatting is what most individuals living without chairs (and toddlers) do every day. This one exercise will improve mobility in the ankle joint, knee, and hip all at once! Most people cannot get into a deep squat position while keeping their heels on the floor, so you can start by hanging on to a pole/doorframe/desk, anything stable and allow yourself to ease into that position and work up to holding a deep squat for 1 minute.

Below is a list of some of the most effective mobility exercises. If you did every exercise on the list, it would only take you 10 minutes! Visit my website, Elevation Enterprise, at www.elevationenterprise.org for videos that demonstrate each of these exercises.

Exercises that are beneficial for increasing mobility:

- Hanging
- Deep squat
- Rocking groin stretch
- Pigeon stretch, rocking
- Downward dog with heel marches
- "World's Greatest Stretch"
- PVC Overhead Pass-throughs
- PVC Good Morning Rotations
- PVC Lat Stretch

Core Strength

"Core training" has become a buzzword in the fitness industry. Most people are aware that strengthening the core muscles is needed on some level. There are books, experts, and even conferences devoted to the topic of core training! However, there is much misleading information presented to the public about what it means to have a strong core. For example, some people equate "toned abs" to a strong core when in actuality, the way your stomach or midsection looks has no relevance to the function of your core! Some people think they must perform hundreds of crunches or sit-ups to build a strong core, although these exercises damage our spinal discs. Some of the misleading information we are given about our core comes from the marketing of useless equipment. The fitness equipment market is full of contraptions claiming that they will "tone and strengthen your core".

For the goal of moving well and feeling great, there are two main responses you want from your core when you train it. Firstly, you want to activate the core muscles you already have! Some people have deactivated their core muscles from lack of use or sitting for most of the day. Secondly, most of the core work you do should promote a "stiff" core. Having stiffness in your core means that your core can stabilize your body from all the rotation that happens in the hips and shoulders (these are our movement joints), and also from outside forces.

The worst exercises you can do for your spine are crunches, rotating ab exercises, or sit-ups. These exercises do not train the core for stiffness or stability, but they do put stress on the spinal discs. The best exercises you can do for the core are listed below. You will notice that many of the exercises involve isometric contractions. This means that there is not movement through the core, rather, we are training it to hold as a pillar of stability. Keep in mind that there are dozens of variations for each of these exercises! Planks for example, can be done on a stability ball, on the floor, using TRX straps, one-handed, one-legged, or while moving a limb/s! Do not try all of these together at once, at least not without a helmet! 😊

Exercises to Develop Core Stability
• Planks and side planks (all variations!)
• Heavy carrying (all variations)
• Hollow holds
• Anti-rotation holds
• Deadbug exercise
• Bird-Dog
• Hard Rolls
• Crawling Patterns

Putting It All Together

Time to put all of the training concepts together! Let's take what we've learned about Cardiovascular Training (levels 1 and 2), Strength Training, Core Activation, Mobility, and Plyometrics, and structure them into a weekly routine! Below is an example of a program to balance your workouts so that you create optimum health, excellent movement, and reduced body age!

Any program, including the one below, needs to be customized for you. Your starting point is going to be determined by several factors such as:

- Your current Level of Activity
- Any existing injuries or areas of limited function
- The types of exercise you've already been doing

For example, if you are already exercising at least 3x/week, you would start a training program at a different point than someone who has not exercised at all in the past few years. A person who is walking or running every day would need to slowly work in interval training and strength training. A person who is lifting 2-3w/week would need to build intervals and mobility into their routine.

If you are not familiar with strength training, I highly recommend that you to hire a personal trainer for a few months to teach you how to properly execute the exercises listed in this chapter. You also could purchase a personalized start-up program from my website, elevationenterprise.org, that will be customized to you. We will take into account your current activity level, whether you have access to gym/no gym, and any injuries/limited movement or health issues you have.

The program outlined below is the goal for you to build yourself up to in a 4- to 6-month period, depending on your starting point. In this program you will be doing a mobility routine 6x/week (3x/week built into your strength training routine, and additional 3x/week as listed).

Weekly Exercise Plan

<u>Day 1:</u>
Strength Training Session (use template below)

<u>Day 2:</u>
Level 1 activity

<u>Day 3:</u>
Mobility routine (5-10 minutes)
Level 2 activity
<u>Day 4:</u>
Strength Training Session

<u>Day 5:</u>
Mobility Routine (5-10 minutes)
Level 1 activity

<u>Day 6:</u>
Strength Training Session

<u>Day 7:</u>
Mobility Routine (5-10 minutes)
Level 2 Activity

Strength Training Template

A great functional strength training session would follow the format below! Refer to the chart of functional exercises given earlier in the chapter to insert in your workout.

1. Warm up with a 5-7-minute Mobility Routine
2. Core Stability Work
   Choose 3-4 exercises from the list of core stability exercises and perform holds of :30-2minutes on each exercise. Do these exercises in a circuit, then repeat the circuit. For example:
   - Side Plank :30 each side
   - Hollow Hold :30
   - Heavy Carry 30 meters
   - REPEAT 2x (for a total of 3 sets)
3. Plyometric work
   Choose 2-3 exercises from the list of plyometrics, and do them in a circuit, resting 2 minutes after the circuit. Repeat 1-2x. For the low impact plyometrics, the reps can be higher such as 20-100. For the high impact plyometrics reps are lower, 5-10. For example:
   - Jump Rope Skips 50x
   - High Knee Jog 20x
   - Box Jumps 5x
   - Rest 2 minutes
4. Superset #1: (repeat 2-3x)
   - Do 4-8 reps of an Upper Body Pull Exercise from the list
   - Rest 60 seconds

- Do 4-8 reps a Back of Lower Body exercise
- Rest 90 seconds

5. Superset #2: (repeat 2-3x)
   - Do 4-8 reps of an Upper Body Push exercise
   - Rest 60 seconds
   - Do 4-8 reps of a Front of Lower Body exercise
   - Rest 90 seconds

> *"Man sacrifices his health to make money, then sacrifices his money to recuperate his health"*
>
> –Dalai Lama

The most common excuse I hear for why people aren't exercising daily is "I don't have time." If this belief or feeling has kept you from exercising in the past, I would like to offer another perspective, a more empowering perspective. Everyone on earth is given the same 24 hours in a day. That is the budget of time allotted to every person; time does not discriminate. It would be truer to say "I haven't made time" instead of "I don't have time".

Some of the busiest, most successful people in the world still make time for intentional exercise every day as they realize that to be and feel their best, they must move!

You can invest 30-60 minutes per day right now to give movement a priority in your life, or you can spend your time and money in a few decades trying to restore your health. You have a choice to make.

Movement is the Holy Grail from which to drink of the fountain of youth. You will look, feel, and live the quality of life you want because you have invested in daily and intentional movement. This is not opinion nor a suggestion, as there are libraries of research proving that every major medical ailment and disease (both mental and physical) show improvement with exercise! Raise your standard from "should" to "must" when it comes to getting some form of exercise every day.

CHAPTER 9:
APPLICATION

"Take Action! An inch of movement will
bring you closer to your goals than a mile of intention."
–Dr. Steve Maraboli

In this book you have learned the secrets to living younger! Knowing what to do and feeling motivated to experience the amazing mental and physical benefits are important. However, you must take **action** to begin enjoying the results!

At the end of this chapter I have summarized a list of daily actions you can start taking that will change your future! You have the power, with each daily action you take, to create an amazing aging experience! I am excited for you to take this power and start creating!

I leave you with a summary of the concepts that create a vibrant mind, body, and spirit through age.

Living Younger Secret 1:
Create an Empowering Mindset
This involves raising your standards for what you can do and who you will be in your later years! You set goals for yourself (and never cease to set new ones), you get role models of people who live decades below their chronological age, you eliminate the "age card",

and you spend time around vibrant people. You start thinking pro-actively and making choices proactively about how to prioritize your time, money, and energy.

Living Younger Secret 2:
Eat Food That Has Life Force In It

You begin eating more food in purest state, freshly picked from the earth, freshly harvested, freshly butchered. You eat more foods with high antioxidant content, you cook with more spices and herbs, and you drink more pure water. You both protect and build up the colonies of helpful bacteria in your gut.

Living Younger Secret 3:
Exercise Daily

This is how you preserve youth in your body! You exercise daily to keep your strength, muscle, mobility, a body that looks good, and also to prevent diseases! You set aside 5-10 minutes per day to do a mobility routine. You have incorporated strength training exercises, plyometrics, and level 1 and level 2 cardio exercises into your weekly routine.

Living Younger Secret 4:
Vibrate Higher

You "fill the glass" each day with higher vibrational emotions such as joy, gratitude, excitement, love, peace, and acceptance. You have forgiven yourself and others. You let go of the lower energies such as anger, blame, hatred, shame, and victimization.

Living Younger Secret 5:
Live with Levity

You sleep longer and more deeply. You play every day, and laugh more often. You eliminate the chronic stress in your life as you feel empowered to leave, change, or accept situations that have robbed you of vitality. You shape a life that you truly enjoy, YOUR life (living proactively).

Activating Youth

Below is summarized list of actions you can take, starting today. Every time you do one of these behaviors, you are increasing your vitality and taking control of your aging experience!

- Go out in nature (as often as possible)
- Go barefoot outside
- Take in sunlight on your skin daily (20 min.)
- Do 1 type of exercise daily (level 1, level 2, mobility work, or strength training)
- Meditate or Pray
- Belly breathe
- Eat foods rich in antioxidants
- Eat food in its natural state at every meal (close to life, full of life-force)
- Eat foods with probiotics in them
- Laugh
- Leave, change, or accept stressful situations
- Sleep deeply, 7-9 hours
- Practice gratitude daily
- Forgive (yourself and others)
- Set goals in writing, and once reached, set new ones
- Raise your expectations for yourself as you age

- Get Role Models! Read their books, watch videos about them, follow them on social media.
- Spend time with proactive people.
- Give special care to your body's communication (pain or discomfort)
- Drink half of your bodyweight (lbs.) in water (ounces)
- Foam roll daily or get a massage 1x/week
- Play!
- Do a 5-10-minute mobility routine each day

Accelerating Aging

The following behaviors will rob years from your body and spirit, rapidly advance the aging process, and make you feel terrible in the process. If you are currently doing any of these things, consider working with a life coach to help you break out of these behavior patterns!

- Sitting for longer than 6 hours/day
- Smoking
- Drinking alcohol other than 8oz red wine
- Drinking soda and/or any beverages with chemical additives
- Drinking more than 16oz coffee
- Daily feeling low energy emotions such as unforgiveness, anger, hatred, depression
- Eating food that is processed or altered (in an unnatural state).

- Staying in chronically stressful life situations
- Using medications to remedy life-style related conditions
- Carrying more than 30lbs of excess weight
- Sleeping less than 7 hours/night
- Lack of play activities and adventure
- Failure to exercise/move

The Living Younger Program

Are you excited to start taking control of your aging experience but don't know where to begin? One resource that can help is our "Living Younger" program. It is an 8-week program that provides you with live coaching and accountability as you begin to make these important life changes—and the best part is it's tailored just for you!

"Our choices determine our destiny"

–A.R. Bernard

By joining, you will get a customized, progressive exercise routine, weekly follow-up from a live coach, and weekly small action steps/ homework in the areas of nutrition, raising vibrations, and creating levity in life. At the end of the 8 weeks you will feel healthier, happier, and more alive! You can find this program on our website elevationenterprise.org. We would love to coach you through these habits!

You can also find printer friendly versions of the food lists and strength training template on our website, www.elevationenterprise.org.

If you have any questions or thoughts that have come to you as you've read this book, we would love to hear from you!

In reading though this book you've learned practical actions you can take that can help you reverse time and aging in your body. I've also exposed you to additional resources for learning about topics that are important but not covered in depth in this book. My hope for you, as you finish reading this book, is that you are left with a greater sense of personal power and a belief in your ability to create a youthful aging experience!

I raise my glass (of water) to you! Drink deeply of youth and enjoy the best life, friends!

ADDENDUM:
HOW TO BELLY BREATHE

Deep, slow, controlled breaths from the diaphragm activate the parasympathetic nervous system, which creates a relaxation response. It also saturates our blood with oxygen! There are numerous physical and phycological benefits resulting from deep breathing practice.

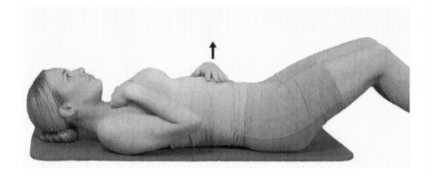

1. Begin lying on your back on a flat surface, head supported by a pillow. Bend your knees (you can place another pillow under your knees for support) and place one hand on your belly and another on your chest to feel your diaphragm as you breathe.
2. Breathe in slowly through your nose, feeling your stomach push against your hand as air fills the deepest point of your lungs. Your chest should remain still.
3. Exhale through your lips while tightening your stomach muscles, letting them fall inward.
4. Repeat for a total of 5 minutes every day. Aim for 3 to 4 times a day for maximum benefits.

BIBLIOGRAPHY

The following references strongly influenced and guided the development of the concepts in this book. Although some of these resources may not be cited specifically, each source provided valuable information, research, and knowledge. Thank you to the following authors, practitioners, and researchers for the insight and expertise you have provided!

Benson, H. M.D. with Miriam Zlipper (1975) *The Relaxation Response.* New York: Harper Collins

Berardi, J. Ph. d (2012) *The Essentials of Sports and Exercise Nutrition Certification Manual.*

Byrne, R. (2006) *The Secret.* Hillsboro, OR: Beyond Words Publishing

Chek, P. (2004) *How to Eat, Move, and Be Healthy.* San Diego, CA: Chek Institute

Cloud, Dr. H. (2010) *Necessary Endings.* New York: Harper-Collins Publisher

Covey, S. (2004) *Seven Habits of Highly Effective People.* New York: Simon and Schuster

Emoto, M. (2004) *The Hidden Messages in Water.* Hillsboro, OR: Beyond Words Publishing

McGill, S. Ph.D. (2015) *Back Mechanic.*

Robbins, T. (1991) *Awaken the Giant Within.* New York: Summit Books

Sisson, M. (2009) *The Primal Blueprint.* Malibu, CA: Primal Nutrition Inc.

Tolle, E. (1991) *The Power of Now.* Vancouver B.C., Canada: Namaste Publishing Inc.

Venuto, T. (2013) *Burn the Fat, Feed the Muscle.* New York: Harmony Books

Morrisey, M. (2016)
https://www.huffingtonpost.com/marymorrissey/the-power-of-writing-down_b_12002348.html

Vitality Tone and Attitude Scale (2006) Stephen J. Cocconi

Tabata, I. (1996) research study
https://www.ncbi.nlm.nih.gov/pubmed/8897392

Simpson, M. (2015) *Difference Between Fitness and Health*
http://www.opt.net.au/difference-fitness-and-health

Lawrence Robinson, M.A., Melinda Smith, M.A., and Robert Segal, M.A. (2018) *Insomnia, what to do when you can't sleep.*
https://www.helpguide.org/articles/sleep/insomnia-causes-and-cures.htm

Mercola, The Ultimate Guide to Antioxidants
https://articles.mercola.com/antioxidants.aspx

ACKNOWLEDGMENTS

The message in this book was birthed out of a desire to pass on goodness to the world, and to empower others to have a more amazing life experience! Thank you to all of my amazing clients at emPower Training Systems, for trusting me with your health, fitness, and lives. I learned a tremendous amount from coaching you and digging deep to figure out how to reach you.

Thank you to the management team at empower Training Systems for being excited for my next steps in life. Thank you USATF, for giving Masters Athletes a platform to perform and compete at high levels, and defy age limitations! Thank you to all my fellow Masters Athletes who set the bar high and showed me how amazing life can be as an older adult.

I would also like to thank my "Circle of Genius" for supporting me during this project. Thank you, Ange, Poppy, and Laura for believing in your friend with big dreams. Thank you, Kendall, for believing in me and my message, and for your support for the process of writing this book. Thank you to my mentor, Cathy, and to the additional launch team members Phil Lapp, Dave Albo, Tovah Koplan, Eric Price, and Dawn Cox. Thank you Dr. Carla Spinelli for being an amazing resource for publishing a book!

Thank you to my three beautiful children, Anya, Elijah, and Grey, who motivate me every day to keep growing and becoming better.

And most importantly, I thank the beautiful, amazing, generous Universe for placing this message in my heart, putting love for others in my soul, and giving me the tenacity and belief in myself to move forward.

ABOUT THE AUTHOR

Angela Myers has been a leader in the fitness industry since 2005, with a passion to help individuals attain their best life. She is a Life Coach, Personal Trainer, and Entrepreneur. She was founder and CEO of an award-winning fitness coaching facility for over a decade. She is a Summa Cum Laude graduate with a B.A. in social work, and remains devoted to continuing education related to wellness, nutrition, the human body, and personal development. She also trains and competes in Masters Track and Field, with several National Titles under her belt.

Angela recently founded Elevation Enterprise, a resource for anyone who wants to cultivate more vitality and fulfillment in their life! She provides personal coaching, speaking engagements, books, programs, and other resources that help you to fuel your body in a way that promotes health, move your body in a way that promotes energy, and develop spiritual wealth and mental/emotional vibrance!

Made in the USA
Middletown, DE
19 November 2019